STORM P

STORM PILOT

The story of the life and leadership
of
GENERAL EDWARD J. HIGGINS
by
WILLIAM HARRIS

Author's manuscript prepared for publication
by Lieut.-Colonel Cyril J. Barnes (R)

Salvationist Publishing and Supplies, Ltd,
Judd Street, King's Cross, London WC1H 9NN

© The Salvation Army, 1981
First published 1981
ISBN 85412 386 5

COLONEL WILLIAM G. HARRIS
became a Salvation Army officer from Brighton, England, in 1920. He served in Indonesia and at International Head-quarters where he was Editor-in-Chief. He retired as Chief Secretary for the USA Eastern Territory, having previously held the same appointment in USA Central. The Colonel was promoted to Glory in 1967.

He is the author of *Stuff that Makes an Army* and *Sagas of Salvationism.*

Printed in Great Britain by The Campfield Press, St Albans

CONTENTS

FOREWORD

IT would have been Utopian to assume that a Movement like The Salvation Army, mushrooming from raw beginnings in the East End of London to an organized and global force for righteousness, should always sail through untroubled waters. In its incipiency there were storms aplenty. Most were external—the misunderstanding of the authorities, civic and ecclesiastical, and the more obvious violence of the mobs.

One storm, however, was internal. With profound regret the Army's leaders in 1929 sought the resignation of their beloved General, Bramwell Booth. Out of the ensuing tempest Edward J. Higgins emerged as the first elected leader of The Salvation Army. No ship riding so close to threatening reefs could have had a steadier hand on the helm than his. God did indeed provide a 'Storm Pilot'.

More than half a century on, the spiritual stature and moral courage of General Higgins is increasingly recognized. Younger Salvationists will read the late Colonel William Harris's biography with avidity and appreciation. Older Salvationists like myself will, while reading, gratefully recollect the General's sensitive statesmanship and his remarkable achievement in successfully bridging two disparate eras of Salvation Army management.

I was privileged to know General Higgins personally. On my shelves are several books he generously gave me. He also gave me words of encouragement and advice, such was my good fortune. And having now sat where he sat, I begin to understand that what he was, what he said and what he did in his day not only strengthened the nerve of his fellow leaders, but also reassured an Army that the God of their fathers was still Commander-in-Chief. This book will remind me to do my best, God helping me, to emulate his sterling example.

Arnold Brown

GENERAL

1

Choice with a challenge

EDWARD HIGGINS made a striking figure as he faced the High Council of The Salvation Army. He had a fine physique and a ruddy countenance, with a mass of greying hair that made him look every inch the leader.

The flashing smile was missing as he weighed his words in deliberate, solemn fashion, but his expressive eyes lent force and deep meaning to every utterance.

There was perhaps the faintest trace of shyness at times in his speech, when he glanced from audience to ceiling, which suggested a winsome humility of spirit; but this gave place to a compelling impression of obvious statesmanship, tried and found true in the furnace of experience, product of a simple discipleship which had placed Jesus Christ as the supreme Personality in his life.

The 63 members of The Salvation Army's first High Council weighed both the man and his words, for theirs was a sacred and important task. Representing all parts of the Army world, they were in conference at Sunbury Court, Sunbury-on-Thames, Middlesex, on Wednesday 13 February 1929, and were to make history and establish a vital precedent in Salvation Army procedures whereby the next General and international leader would be chosen by election of the Council rather than by appointment from his predecessor.

For 37 days the High Council had experienced periods of exceptional strain on emotions and minds, relieved only by memorable devotional periods fraught with great spiritual power and fellowship, as matters vital to the well-being and leadership of the world's only international army were weighed, emphasized and decided upon.

Now the time had come for the election of the new General.

Stormy days were these in the Army world, alive with problems which gripped the interest of millions of people from Hyderabad to

Houndsditch, and sent Salvationists of every race to their knees in prayer that God would guide the selection of a pilot for the storm.

Evangeline Booth had spoken and it was now the turn of Edward J. Higgins.

Of the two final nominees for leadership not a few favoured Higgins as the man of their choice. Yet his speech was not one designed to seek votes even if it won them.

'I think I should say to you frankly that I shall not be disappointed if I am not elected General,' he commenced. 'My plans have been made for over a year now and were made known to the General at that time, by which I fully intended to retire from active service on the attainment of my 65th year. . . .

'If I were left to consider my own feelings and were to follow the inclinations of my heart and mind, I should still plead that these plans be allowed to mature: but it has been expressed to me by one and another in this room that it would be hardly "playing the game" if I were to shrink from bearing some of the burdens which present conditions impose on Salvation Army leaders.'

This was hardly the anticipated opening of an address from a nominee for the Generalship, and the fact did not become less plain as the speaker continued in those clear, deep, resonant tones which later became world famous:

'I have therefore yielded to those views to the extent that I have not asked that my name should be removed from the list of nominees; and wish now to say that after much prayer and the seeking of guidance, I am willing to do my best for you all and for the Army, if it is clear by the voting which presently will follow that the bulk of the council desires me for the post.

'But I should say that whilst the Deed Poll requires a two-thirds majority to elect a General, I shall not allow my name to go to any further ballot after it has been revealed by voting that a majority, *however small*, desires someone else. I could not, of course, myself transfer votes to anyone, but I must then be reckoned out of the running.'

Edward Higgins then felt it necessary to state his views clearly on matters disturbing the minds of Army leaders, so that no vote would

2

be given him under any false impression. He was anxious not to be considered as a leader of a 'reform' party.

It was nearly midnight when the President of the Council, Commissioner James Hay, announced that Edward J. Higgins had been elected by 42 votes to 17, a sufficient majority to place him in supreme command of the Army.

To a background of affectionate acclaim from his comrades, he signed the Deed of Acceptance, the same being witnessed by William Frost, the Army's solicitor, thus the Army received its third General, and the first not to bear the honoured name of Booth.

Characteristic of the man, Edward Higgins made no impressive speech that night. Instead, his words were brief and courteous, expressing thanks and appreciation. He sensed the great responsibility which had fallen on his shoulders.

Hastening home, his first act was one of prayer. The Army's new leader cried to God for His wisdom and help and soon afterwards said:

'I should despair if I did not think God heard my cry. If I walk humbly before Him I have confidence that He will be my sufficiency and day by day make me equal to the demands that are made upon me.'

Edward Higgins met High Council members the following morning. He addressed them for the first time as their General and heard leading officers pledge their loyalty, as well as their determination to carry forward the Army's work with aims and purposes unchanged, and to engage Salvationists everywhere in a new holy crusade for God and righteousness.

The Salvation Army's first High Council had been held; a new chapter of Army history had been commenced and Edward J. Higgins was the chief scribe.

2

Son of Somerset

AS a Somerset man, Edward J. Higgins loved the Mendip Hills of England. 'Though I travel the countries of the world,' he often said, 'when I hear the broad burr of the Somerset dialect—it sounds like music.' Born at 10 Church Street, Highbridge, on 26 November 1864, he was a small town boy who became a citizen of the world.

Eight months before William Booth started the work of The Christian Mission, which later became The Salvation Army, Edward John was born to Edward and Martha Higgins, the first boy and third child of a family of eight (five of whom died in infancy). He was named Edward after his father, and John after his uncle John Buskin, founder and prominent member of the local Wesleyan Methodist chapel.

The father was a saddler and kept a shop which formed part of a small house in which the family lived, a nondescript dwelling, a unit in a row of lowly homes set along a narrow pavement. The shop opened on to the street and the living rooms were to the rear. Upstairs were the shallow bedrooms, partially built over a dark passage which led to a limited back garden. Here was a well with an old iron pump and a flower garden, the special joy of mother Martha.

She was the only daughter of George Deacon, a Highbridge man. Her delicate health rarely allowed her to leave home and garden, save sometimes to go to chapel. Nevertheless, she gave unstintingly of her waning strength to the care and training of her large family, with such a beautiful spirit that 70 years afterwards she remained vivid in the memory of her son Edward. Said he: 'Her words sound in my ears, and her life shines before me as a beacon and blessing.'

On Sunday nights she would gather her family into the sitting-room and read to them from the Bible, or encourage the older children to learn stories from Bunyan's *Pilgrim's Progress*. During

4

these intimate hours—pleasing and congenial at the time and un-speakably precious thereafter—Edward was instructed in principles that were to prove throughout his life as immovable as mountains.

The children said their prayers at mother's knee and were always safely put to bed before father returned from chapel. When mother was able, she attended the morning service and sometimes Edward accompanied her. Even in those days he remembers forming definite opinions concerning preachers, and the foundations of his religious beliefs were well and truly laid.

The father—Edward senior—came from a family of ardent Methodists with puritanical leanings not too congenial to a young man. Eventually he rebelled, and for a time 'ran rather wild', as the villagers said. Then he married lovely Martha Deacon, who brought into his life an influence for good, and inspired a spiritual develop-ment which made him so zealous a champion for right and an exceptional toiler for God.

As a small boy Edward junior attended the Sunday-school at the Highbridge Wesleyan Chapel, and since many of the visiting preachers came to his home for meals, one of his boyhood privileges was a personal contact with some of the robust stalwarts of Methodism.

In Higgins' home, amid the pungent odours of leather and saddle soap and the dank smell of tan, Edward spent the happy hours of early boyhood.

Two miles from Highbridge is the town of Burnham-on-Sea, where, as a toddler of four, Higgins started his education at Simon Harris's school, and early became a sturdy walker as he trudged 20 miles a week in his journeyings to and from the classroom.

A few months after his eighth birthday he was met one day at the school gate by Uncle John Ruskin, and as they walked home it dawned on the lad that something serious or important had happened. Before the pair reached home Uncle John had broken the heart-breaking news that the boy's mother had died. The care and anxiety of a quickly-arriving family had proved too great a strain on the woman's weak frame, and the birth of her last child had brought about her death. She was 33 years of age.

Thus on a cold, snowy day in March 1873, Edward, with his father and sisters (his only brother had died), followed the casket to the Wesleyan chapel, and after a simple service his mother was taken to the Burnham-on-Sea parish church of St Andrews for burial. Young Edward was left with a piteous sense of loss and desolation.

Details of the service, conducted by a local preacher of the circuit, soon faded from his memory, but the influence of his mother remained with him, an indelible impression on heart and mind for ever. In after years he realized and admired her positive attitude to life and the way she had held up goodness as the healthy, normal, wholesome, worth-while way of living. Although she had never chastised, she had invariably made her point.

In private conversation and in public utterance Edward Higgins often thanked God for his mother. When as a lad he was tempted to take advantage of a friend, to tell a lie or to speak thoughtlessly, mother's memory challenged him to be an overcomer.

Edward went to live with his maternal grandfather, while his father, crushed by the blow of his wife's passing and overburdened by efforts to keep going his none-too-prosperous business, gave up the struggle in Highbridge and moved to Bridgwater, nine miles away, where he bought a boot and shoe store and in the course of time married again. Business flourished and additional shops were opened and after a while he settled in Reading.

In Reading something happened which transformed his life, and he became the associate of Isaac Palmer, the 'biscuit man' (of the internationally known firm of Huntley and Palmer), as a militant temperance advocate. As such Edward Higgins senior was in frequent demand as a speaker.

Grandfather Deacon was now responsible for Edward junior's education and the boy owed much to the older man's progressive thinking and passionate desire to give him the best possible education.

He went to two schools. First to a small private school in Burnham, with its spare-time teacher, a lame man, who also carried the local mail. Then to Dr Morgan's Grammar School at Bridgwater, one with considerable status in the county. He became a boarder in the house of the headmaster, Dr Lucette, but was generally permitted week-end leave to Highbridge.

At this time there was little to distinguish Edward Higgins from the 200 other boys of the school, with their high hats, long striped

6

trousers, short cut-away coats and expansive Eton collars. Cricket was his favourite sport. He revelled in it and learned to 'play the game' in the best sense of the phrase. In studies he was rated slightly above average, became one of the two best readers of the school, liked mathematics, found languages difficult but was fascinated by every high standard of penmanship.

To the disappointment of his grandparents, music was not among Edward's good subjects. He blamed a schedule which detailed him for piano practice at 5.45 each morning. No teachers were about at that hour and the cold mornings created no passion for the arts. Moreover, none knew how faithful or correct he was in his exercises. He himself admitted that he did not overdo things musically and when the next lad came to the piano at 6.30 he always surrendered the bench with relief and alacrity.

'As a boy', said Edward Higgins to a newspaper man years afterwards, 'I never was naughty enough to commit any crime, and never good enough to be noticed as one likely to achieve any greatness! I was, in fact, a mediocrity.'

Grandfathers sometimes supply a clue to the inner characters of their grandchildren. John Deacon, for instance, was noted for his punctuality. He was the chief clerk of a coal-yard and people set their clocks by his comings and goings. Certainly, Edward Higgins loved to be on time. When he came to positions of leadership he was always keen that a meeting should start never a moment later than the time announced.

In the same way, traits of leadership seen in the grandfather showed themselves in the grandson, for the older man was progressive, had decided views and was much sought after by his neighbours for advice in both family and business matters.

He was also that kind of man who believed that it is always in season for old men to learn, for when Edward came home from school each Friday night, it was the grandfather's great interest to catechize him on the lessons of the week—not merely as a check on the boy's progress, but to satisfy his own unquenchable thirst for knowledge.

During one of these week-ends at home, a veritable spiritual firebrand came to Highbridge, a Methodist local preacher named Thomas Perrett; and since all the Higgins' relatives attended the

Wesleyan Methodist chapel, they came under the preacher's compelling power and holy enthusiasm. On Sunday morning his trenchant words shook the pious complacency of his hearers as he declared the truth in a manner as unorthodox as it was unusual. Eyes opened wide when he announced that an open-air meeting would be held before the evening service. This was an innovation, and a large crowd attended to watch the preacher conduct the meeting single-handed, then march, a procession of one, to the chapel.

Later it was learned that Perrett had received a 'baptism of fire' at the recently-opened Salvation Army corps at Bridgwater. As an evangelist of the flaming heart he poured out his soul in passionate appeal for men and women to seek Christ as their Saviour. Young Higgins, 14 years old, was greatly impressed. At the close of the meeting 17 people knelt at the communion rail. Edward Higgins was among them!

The preacher's words had made him realize that he was not converted. The joyous religion of his mother was not his; and he sought it. He was conscious of his sin and knew himself to be in rebellion against God. Maybe no one would have described his sins as vile, but the boy realized they separated him from God and he wanted to be a Christian as his mother had been. True, he had sung at times in the chapel choir, but he wanted to give a better service. He realized, though in a way that was somewhat vague, that the Lord had a right to his life and affections.

No one spoke to the kneeling lad, but the memory of his mother's words and wishes guided him, as with genuine sorrow he repented of all he knew to be wrong and by faith claimed the saving grace of Jesus Christ.

Throughout the years the actual date of the glorious experience eluded him, but on that Sunday evening he knew he had become a new lad in Christ Jesus. Without delay he wrote to tell his father.

By nature Edward was inclined to be quiet and reserved, but Thomas ('The Fiery') Perrett greatly appealed to him. From the start he knew that his was to be no quiet religion. He must pass on the good news.

Next morning he faced his companions at school and in a husky voice, somewhat shyly, told them what had happened the night before. Some smiled, others appeared indifferent, a few became

8

interested. For the remainder of his school life he was appraised and watched by almost everyone. His headmaster, Dr Lucette, became his guide, encouraging and helping the young student in his early Christian experience.

At Highbridge, Edward became a Sunday-school teacher, attended the class meetings regularly and learned to pray aloud.

Before he was 15 he passed the Oxford Local Examination with honours, left school and went to work for Nathaniel Harding, a Highbridge provision merchant, although Grandfather Deacon wanted him to become a lawyer, or a publisher, and was making plans for his further education.

3

Army of the Lord

THE year 1881 found The Salvation Army one of the great sensations of Britain's larger cities. Its unorthodox methods shocked the churches and its courageous Christianity stirred the forces of evil to mass their mobs in cruel, unreasonable, violent persecution and opposition.

But the Army proved to be the simple, sincere vehicle of the living God to the degraded, hopeless and pitiful masses of the nation's poor. Miracles happened. Outcasts were transformed into citizens. The harlot sought Christ; the penitent thief became the potent preacher; drunkards were made sober.

Such remarkable conversions greatly interested Edward's father. This form of religion was what his town, Reading, needed. Therefore he pleaded with William Booth to send officers. 'I promise you', he wrote, 'to render all the help I posssibly can to establish a corps.'

General Booth responded. A large disused boat-house on the riverbank was fitted out for the meetings, and the first Sunday, 27 March, was a memorable one. 'The processions were enormous, and the interest evoked considerable,' reported *The War Cry* a few days later. 'The roughs, however, were in strong force and our two officers were roughly handled by the mob, but providentially escaped out of their hands.'

Although Major William Day, the leader for the Army's Southern Division, and Captain Charles Harrison were reasonably safe, one of the chief objects of the mob's fury was Higgins senior. Was he not the one local person responsible for the Army's advent?

The crowd rushed to his home and became so threatening that the mayor read the Riot Act and the military were called to clear the streets; but not until blood had flowed freely and the windows of the Higgins' dwelling had been smashed with stones and sticks. The officers still wanted to hold a meeting that night, but the police would not allow them.

Nevertheless, after receiving such a brutal initiation into Salvation Army warfare, the Reading businessman resolved to become a Salvationist, and the news rang through the town that Higgins was the new organization's first recruit. His boot and shoe business suffered for a while, for people were afraid to visit the shop or to associate with anyone favouring these strange Salvationist people, but he had faith that God was leading him, and he gave every spare moment to the work of the Army.

Soon Reading Salvationists knew the joy of taking part in a great revival. Hundreds of people were converted in the old boat-house. True there was no comfort in the crude seats, rain came through the roof and mother earth was the floor; yet night after night eager crowds filled the place and some of the town's worst people accepted the Christian faith.

At that time and during the succeeding years, the elder Higgins marched at the head of Army processions, and with his conspicuous tall figure and high hat became a stately objective for the filth and missiles of the mob. He never showed a quiver of fear. At the Army hall he would calmly scrape and clean his clothes to make himself as presentable as possible for the platform. He became the hero of the younger Salvationists who also gloried in the scars of the battle.

The War Cry of 7 April 1881 carried the following report:

> We have had 127 souls since last Wednesday. . . . This town is moved from end to end. Yesterday . . . the salvation boat-house was crowded all day. . . . This morning one of the ringleaders of last Sunday's work came and cried to me, begging for pardon. Of course, I forgave him. (From Captain Harrison.)

Two months later Reading Corps received a week-end visit from William Booth to inspect the rapidly progressing work and to present that corps' first flag. On the Saturday afternoon Salvationists gathered at the railway station to receive the General, then marched through the town led by a band of brass and string instrumentalists. This was reported as 'an event which interested everybody, pleased most, possibly disgusted some and certainly did good to a great many'.

All these things and many more were related in letters from father to son, and the younger Edward thrilled to the crusading adventure of it all and desired to know more of the Army for himself.

During that visit to Reading William Booth saw in the elder Higgins a man who could be of great service in his rapidly growing organization, and before the end of the year asked him to give up his business and join him at the headquarters in London. It was a great thing to ask, but after much prayer Higgins accepted the conditions for entering the service and arrived in London for his first appointment on 9 January 1882.

Thus started a distinguished career which took Edward Higgins senior to Commissioner's rank in the Army and wrote his name large in the Organization's saga of service.

When William Booth visited Bristol for the week-end of 4 to 6 February 1882, for a 'council of war' he took the Colston Hall and Staff-Captain Higgins (as he had become) was instructed to be present.

Highbridge was but 30 miles away and father Higgins saw an opportunity to introduce his son to the Movement he had joined. It was a 'full dress' week-end, for William and Catherine Booth were accompanied by members of their family, who were attractions in themselves.

The dense fog in London which had caused William to miss his pre-arranged train at Paddington was soon forgotten and the Colston Hall presented a scene of siege as a crowd of 2,000 struggled unsuccessfully to enter an already overcrowded building.

Young Edward had never seen anything like this—people fighting their way to church. Using a little initiative and persuasion, he gained admittance by way of the stage door. There were no seats available, only uncomfortable standing room. But he was in, and that was all that mattered. He found himself near the platform. The great audience amazed him and the singing moved him deeply.

Meetings continued throughout the week-end, when this singing was accompanied by the Fry family band from Salisbury. Captain George Fielder sang the recently-written words, 'Bless His name, He sets me free', to the tune of 'Champagne Charlie'. The Captain had sung it at his own corps of Worcester when William Booth had visited the city a few weeks before, and the Army's Founder had changed his mind in favour of using music hall tunes with religious words.

Florence Soper, later that year to become Mrs Bramwell Booth, spoke of her conversion under the guidance of Miss Emma Booth. Captain James Wookey was called in from Cradley Heath to tell of his deliverance from being 'a drunken wretch'.

Mrs Booth's words were awe-inspiring as she logically and with great force pleaded the cause of her Lord. The Founder spoke in a spirit of dynamic abandon to the will of God. He talked of sin, judgement, heaven and hell, of salvation and damnation; and then invited the unsaved to the Mercy Seat.

The atmosphere was charged with spiritual power. It was no surprise to the younger Edward to see the crowds in each meeting making their way to the Penitent-form; his wonder was that everybody did not come.

He was not only deeply stirred in mind and spirit; he was challenged. All through the night he fought a spiritual battle. Should these Salvationists—his father's people—be his people? Should his future be in The Salvation Army? What about his career? Countless questions projected themselves and demanded answers.

His grandfather had offered him the ways and means to qualify as a lawyer or a publisher; he could make his choice. It was a tempting offer and this was the Sunday of the very week he had promised to give a definite answer. In Highbridge the answer had been obvious; but Bristol had changed everything. A new attraction had presented itself. Winning souls for Christ now seemed to be the most important thing in life.

But there were strong arguments to be considered. His father had told him that there was no guarantee of salary. There was little social position. The Movement was despised. Had not the persecuting mob at Reading shown this?

Away from the great crowd and the soul-stirring singing, the outlook seemed dark and unattractive. Certainly there was the memory of wonderful prayers and those deeply moving scenes at the Mercy Seat; but there was the price to pay of being despised, persecuted and treading paths of loneliness.

Then, as the rays of the morning sun shone their way over the

13

distant horizon, Higgins made his decision. On the lonely unattractive path that seemed his future in the Army, he saw a Cross and the vision of Him who hung upon it for the sins of the world. The light dawned. His duty became obvious, and he surrendered to the claims of God. An indescribable joy possessed him. After the week-end he set off to catch an early train for home, to tell his grandfather the startling news.

Although Higgins senior was a Staff-Captain at headquarters, the family home was still at Reading, where Edward's stepmother was clearing up the affairs of his father's business. In March 1882 the son went to live there and became a soldier of the Reading Corps.

Here he learned new lessons in Army warfare on a hard training ground. The boy's naturally reserved disposition fought shy of publicity and resented ridicule; but he was greatly helped by a faithful soldier, 'Happy Freddie Lea', who regularly called at his house and went with him to the open-air meetings. Here he made his first efforts to speak in public. Although the howling mob stood all around, he was urged to be a good soldier and say something. This he did but always doubted if anyone heard a word he said because of the noise of the crowd.

The new soldier was not permitted to shirk any part of his duties. Edward Higgins often said in after years that his humble soldier friend did more than anyone else in those early days to help him adventure into the 'rough and tumble' of Salvation Army warfare.

Before he donned full uniform he wore an Army shield on his coat. Even that was enough to attract the attention of passers-by, and he was called all sorts of names by the roughs wherever he turned.

While Edward was still a new soldier the famous Clapton Congress Hall and Training Home was opened in May 1882, and he travelled to London for some of the special meetings. Here he received great help and inspiration and made a definite offering of himself for officership.

Interviewed by Bramwell Booth, Chief of the Staff, he was told that 'another year's experience as a soldier would be helpful', but Higgins could see no necessity for such a delay and so ably pleaded his cause that he was allowed to fill in the necessary candidate's forms at once.

14

He now took every opportunity to gain experience for the future, but with between four and five hundred fiery young converts in the corps a dozen of them were invariably in the open-air ring waiting for a chance to speak. He had to fight for a chance to make his witness.

All through his life Edward Higgins remembered the first time he spoke in an inside meeting on a Sunday night. 'I had been told beforehand that my officer was going to call on me,' he wrote years later, 'and, oh, the agony I suffered! I had prayed and prepared most carefully, but got on very poorly. I stumbled and stuttered, and at last sat down, feeling in my heart that I would never do it again.' Nevertheless he did try again and made the most of his opportunities. He became a sergeant and acting corps treasurer. He also took charge of an outpost at nearby Twyford.

His service as a soldier was short-lived for orders to enter training were received on Monday 4 September 1882, and, still only 17, Cadet Edward Higgins entered the portals of the training home in Clapton.

4

A fighter in the Field

IF challenges accepted make a champion, and struggles are the secret of strength, then the early officership experiences of Edward J. Higgins played an important role in providing the Army's third General.

The 1880s were days when the leadership demands of the Army were great enough to compel men and women to be rushed to the command of forces in the field with often only short and meagre training. Preparation at the 'School of the Prophets', the name given by a writer of the day to the training home at Linscott Road, Clapton, sometimes consisted of only a few weeks. In 1882 there were about 200 cadets in residence, who were commissioned according to their readiness and the exigencies of the war.

'I was in the training home 13 weeks,' Higgins wrote. 'Somehow, I do not fancy they thought very much of me. I was still so nervous and I fear they felt me to be stand-offish.'

But the hurly-burly of training, with its emphasis on practice rather than theory, helped him. In common with cadets of the 1880s he had many unpleasant experiences, especially in connection with open-air evangelism. The Salvation Army waged its unrelenting war against sin and many were the vicious counter-attacks by the forces of evil. It was a rough business. The cadets were frequently attacked by the mob. Clothes were spoiled and black eyes and physical injuries were common. The neighbouring corps such as Hackney, Stoke Newington, Whitechapel, Limehouse, Poplar and Bethnal Green, were battlegrounds. Sometimes the rowdies prevented the cadets marching and on occasions they had to cover their uniforms in order to reach Clapton in safety.

In the training home Cadet Higgins was occupied most of the time with clerical duties. Major T. Henry Howard, the vice-principal, was acting treasurer of the Clapton Congress Hall Corps, but Higgins attended to most of the details of the work. He was also

16

appointed librarian of the small but growing library at the training home and was made responsible for the distribution and the resulting cash income of the cadets' *War Cry* sales.

Outstanding in the training home curriculum were lectures and 'spiritual days' by General William Booth and the Army Mother (Mrs Catherine Booth). From these impressive occasions Cadet Higgins imbibed the principles of salvationism.

In September 1882 William Booth acquired the notorious Grecian Theatre in Hoxton, London, when 6,000 people crowded to the first day's meetings. These were occasions of fierce opposition—both inside and outside the building; but often in the midst of the most unbecoming tumult the Penitent-form would be lined again and again with many of the people who had come to disturb. These were memorable moments for the young man who had been attracted to the Army by its soul-saving zeal.

Cadet Higgins sometimes found himself on duty in the topmost gallery of the Grecian to keep order among the roughest and the toughest. Often, however, when the proceedings were boisterous and rowdyism seemed to reign supreme, the voice of the tempter would whisper: 'You're not cut out for this sort of thing. You belong to a different class of people. You have mistaken your calling. You are in the wrong place!' But prayer carried the young warrior through to victory.

Edward Higgins learned the secret of prayer from the practical lectures on the subject by Catherine Booth. Said he concerning a day of extreme discouragement: 'Such light came to me as she spoke. She talked on lines which comforted me; made me anxious to pray for a deeper love for souls and to be willing to sacrifice if only I might become a soul-winner. . . . I remember so well as the lecture closed I went up to my dormitory and settled the question, deciding in my heart as never before, "Come what may I am going through". . . . Of course, Mrs Booth never knew what she had done for me, but I shall always thank God for her words.'

Before Higgins became used to the 'training harness' he was selected for a field appointment. A campaign for the establishment of new corps in Great Britain had been planned for the first week of December 1882, and he was one of the 101 cadets commissioned by General William Booth in the Exeter Hall, some of whom were sent to open these new centres.

17

Edward, as Lieutenant, and his Captain, Philip Kyle, were commissioned among the 101 and were appointed to the Durham City Corps. They arrived on a bitterly cold and windy night, with the snow falling heavily. Their quarters, a small cottage (one room up and down), was in a dismal court known as 'Reform Place'. The hall, a most uninviting building, was centrally situated, but in the dark cellar of a chemist's shop by the riverside. A warm-hearted soldiery, however, soon made the outlook more encouraging.

The new officers had not been in Durham City long before they became the object of criticism by Dr Joseph B. Lightfoot, the then Bishop of Durham, but they refused to be drawn into the argument. It was Kyle's announced sermon topic, 'Lost in the eternal snows of Hell', that irritated the bishop. Be that as it may, it must be remembered that the same Church leader had already, a fortnight after the new officers' arrival, called his clergy to be friendly to the Salvationists and to read their books. In his charge he had urged them:

> Shall we be satisfied with going on as hitherto, picking up one here and one there, gathering together a more or less select congregation, forgetful meanwhile of the Master's command, 'Go out into the highways and hedges, and compel them to come in'? The Salvation Army has taught us a higher lesson than this. Whatever may be its faults, it has at least called us to this lost ideal of the work of the Church—the universal compulsion of the souls of men.

Crowds thronged to the Army meetings. The basement hall normally accommodated 200 people but often 450 were present. It became necessary to hire the town hall for Sunday afternoon and evening services, using the Army hall for overflow gatherings.

Kyle and Higgins were inveterate workers; no task was too heavy, no hours too long. Soul-saving was their chief delight and God gave them the joy of winning many. How the soldiers and the ordinary people loved them!

Edward Higgins led his first soul to Christ at Durham on the Sunday afternoon after his arrival there. She was Emma Askew, who became the wife of Commissioner William McAlonan. Margaret Harwood, who became Mrs Lieut.-Commissioner Charles Duce, and served in Japan and India, was also a young person in Durham City Corps.

A lad of 11, greatly impressed by Higgins' ministry, also was converted at this time and became not only the treasurer of the corps but a justice of the peace and Lord Mayor of Durham City, Alderman John W. Pattinson.

Many trophies of grace were among the converts, including 'Dad' Gray, a gas company employee, saved through Higgins' pub-booming; 'Happy Sally', a slave to drink who became the corps colour sergeant; 'Lanky Jack', who revelled in advertising the corps meetings by carrying sandwich boards; Mother Vasey, who delighted to do all she could for her 'Teddy', as she called the Lieutenant; and George Wardle, who before conversion drank his beer from a bucket and slept off his drunken stupor in the outhouses of the neighbourhood.

The young officers made systematic visitation an important part of their plans in following up and shepherding their converts. A simple card system indicated clearly if a convert was absent from a meeting and it only required a man or woman to miss two week-night meetings for the officers to be on his doorstep in anxious inquiry.

Selling copies of *The War Cry* and *The Young Soldier* in the public-houses has been a typical Salvation Army form of evangelism down through the years. Early in his career Edward Higgins recognized the power of the Army's periodicals in bringing Christ to the non-church-going people. Kyle and Higgins were enthusiastic evangelists of the printed word. *The War Cry* was published each Wednesday and Saturday and Durham City's total weekly sales were over 2,000. Many miles were trudged; there were no cheap cycles in those days. They knew that sermons might fade, but the printed word would remain.

Higgins of those days was described by Alderman Pattinson as 'very methodical, a terrific worker, devoted to both corps and out-post work, a good man for the young people, thorough in visitation, with soul-saving always his chief concern. As a speaker he was timid but racy. He was not inclined to humour, straight in his dealings, rather independent and liked to carry his own bag. In physique he was well built, strong, agile, with a fair complexion and rosy face, blue eyes. He was handsome.' His natural reserve and gentlemanly demeanour attracted many people of his own kind to the Army.

Through the generosity of Alderman James Fowler, the first Durham City Band was formed during the time of Kyle and Higgins. Out of the 150 converts who had been won in a few weeks it seemed

19

an excellent idea to form a band to provide a useful outlet of service. Public interest was sought and 20 new instruments were purchased. In due course they arrived amid scenes of great excitement.

After one of the meetings the Captain asked the male members of the corps to stay behind. They were requested to raise their hands if they knew anything about music. Not a hand was uplifted, so it was for the best-looking men to be chosen for the band. Kyle and Higgins were determined to have at least an aggregation of handsome instrumentalists.

The 20 new instruments which had just been bought were handed out according to size, basses to the bigger men and cornets to the smaller, with the adjuration, 'Get to know something about music and this instrument as soon as possible.'

The next night the band played in public! The noise was terrible. If the melody was 'There is a happy land', it was certainly very 'far away' from Durham City. Nevertheless, the leader of the band was a little put out that his officers did not recognize the tune.

After six months' service in Durham City, crowned with success and with next to no opposition, save minor disturbances by gamblers and roughs, the two officers received orders to move to Darlington.

In Darlington, where a corps had been established four years earlier, Edward Higgins served under two Captains—three months with Philip Kyle and the same period with George Braine. Both made major contributions to his development. Kyle was vigorous, studious, an early riser, planned each day carefully and taught his Lieutenant to love work and to appreciate its true value. Braine, who had once been a blacksmith, had close fellowship with him in prayer and taught the great value of petition and its effect on both life and work.

The soul-saving scenes of Durham City were repeated in Darlington. Huge crowds filled the Livingstone Hall on Sundays and the Mercy Seat was lined again and again with men and women seeking Christ as Saviour. Men of public repute associated themselves with the work and gave valued assistance. Land was secured for a new building.

United divisional meetings led by Major James Dowdle taught the Lieutenant many valuable things. Dowdle, who was famous for his violin playing and daring tactics used in evangelism, and who became a Commissioner, invariably had a private word with each officer before he returned to his post. He spoke in the most intimate and friendly way of the spiritual experience each should enjoy.

Six months in Darlington (the average stay of a corps officer in the early days of the Army) was followed by a short period among the all-alive Irish soldiery of Ballymacarrett, before a surprise appointment to assist Captain Kyle again, this time at Oldham 1. A large skating rink was regularly packed for the meetings. Five hundred soldiers attended the seven o'clock knee-drills (early morning prayer meetings) on Sundays and nearly 500 soldiers, mostly uniformed, marched to the open-air meetings.

These gatherings were deeply-moving experiences, for the stirring testimonies of converts who were formerly drunkards, thieves, wife-beaters and ne'er-do-wells were used by the Holy Spirit to help win others of their kind.

When William Booth visited Oldham, Lieutenant Higgins was assigned to show the great man the way to an open-air meeting. During a 20-minute walk, William Booth, ever skilled as a counsellor, opened up to him visions of what the Army was destined to be and the opportunities it would give him to serve Jesus Christ. He also advised him on the kind of books he should read and how best to train his heart and mind for the future.

As they reached the place for the open-air meeting the General suddenly dropped to his knees and, placing his hand on the young officer, who had knelt by his side, blessed him in the name of the Lord. He prayed that his life should be filled with holy service.

Before Higgins was 20 years of age he was promoted to the rank of Captain, on receipt of orders to establish a corps in Kettering. In Christian Mission days a station had been formed but was later abandoned. Nevertheless some of the earlier supporters welcomed the advent of the Army.

From the start crowds attended the meetings, held in a long auctioneer's mart. There was no rush of penitents, but every week men and women knelt at the Mercy Seat and, when Captain Higgins farewelled after a four-month stay, he left behind a Salvationist fighting force of over 100. He also established the nucleus of a corps in the nearby town of Rothwell.

5

Extending battlefield

FOLLOWING this brief but successful period as a corps officer Edward Higgins was promoted to the rank of Staff-Captain and appointed ADC to Major George Kilby, divisional officer for the Leicester and Northampton Division, where he became engaged in clerical and business routine and had direct responsibility for village expansion work in two counties. Long trudges through the country-side, day after day, to hamlets far from a railway station, was challenging but exhausting work for the young man still under 21.

A year of such activity took its physical toll. Not even the care of the Kilbys, the happiness of their home and the devoted care they gave to the young ADC, prevented a serious breakdown. Cessation from work became imperative and Higgins went to seek renewed health at Folkestone.

These were days of temptation. It seemed illogical that a young man who had given life and prospects to God, and who had served the cause of the Army with such zeal and energy, should find himself apparently at the end of living before life had scarcely begun.

He trusted the leadings of God implicitly and, to the surprise of many, in six months Staff-Captain Higgins was able to report for duty once more. The General was concentrating on capturing the lost of London and had planned the opening of many new corps. A provincial officer was appointed to command the greater London area with five divisional officers working under his direction, each with roving commissions for certain areas. Higgins was appointed divisional officer for South-West London.

When Edward Higgins senior, now assuming positions of greater responsibility in the Army, found his work taking him to Wales, he was frequently billeted at the home of David Price, building con-tractor of Penarth, near Cardiff. What was more natural for a proud father than to speak of the work of his son? Interest was aroused by the glowing accounts, by Edward's prospects, not forgetting his good looks. Catherine, the eldest child, showed an interest by no means least in the family.

Catherine pioneered salvationism in the Price home. True, the father, a Baptist, had taken his daughter to see and hear 'those queer people' when The Salvation Army opened fire in Penarth, but he hardly bargained that the Army would win his 14-year-old daughter and that she in turn would lead the family into Blood-and-Fire service.

From the first Sunday-night meeting she attended, Catherine Price was attracted to the Salvationists and their work. On the following Tuesday night she was at the meeting again and then on every possible occasion. Yet it was not until 12 December 1882 that she surrendered to Christ at the Penitent-form. Thereafter she became a fighting soldier of the Army.

Open-air meetings especially were her delight in company with a large group of young people who joined the corps. Night after night many of them rushed direct from their employment, never troubling even to change from their working clothes.

Catherine's mother had died when she was but two years and she was raised by a stepmother. Mrs Price was against her daughter becoming a Salvationist, but since the father supported the work her protests were short-lived. Eventually David Price also joined the Army and became treasurer of Penarth Corps.

Catherine attended school at Chard and proudly wore her Salvation Army pin, speaking freely and naturally to her friends of her new experience in Christ and of the unique nightly happenings at the Army. Some of the girls made fun of her and mimicked Salvation Army mannerisms and unconventionalities, while the school principal expressed her surprise and horror that a daughter of Mrs Price should associate with such 'scum'. Catherine remained undisturbed.

God was working out His plan for her life. When she left school and her officers encouraged her to full-time service and closer contact with the Organization, she served as a Sub-Lieutenant in Blaina and then in Aberdare, before entering the training home at 17 years of age.

After serving in a number of corps, each for a short time, she was appointed as Captain to Teddington, in the South-West London

Division, where the divisional officer was Staff-Captain Edward Higgins.

It was not quite 'love at first sight' but Catherine Price and Edward Higgins were quickly attracted to each other. The first time she ever saw him was at a united meeting in the Clapton Congress Hall, and the first time they met was on a train going to Feltham, travelling with a group of officers; but she left the train before he did.

Captain Price was late for her first officers' council in the division, held at Hammersmith, and received a reproving look from the young divisional officer as she entered the hall. Nevertheless Staff-Captain Higgins was not slow to admit that his heart went out strangely to Captain Catherine Price.

About this time Bramwell Booth, Chief of the Staff, was talking to the Staff-Captain.

'Are you engaged, Higgins?' he asked.

'No, sir, not yet,' came the reply.

'Would you like me to help you by way of some introductions to meet the right young woman?'

'Well, thank you, sir,' came the rather embarrassed reply. 'Thank you, sir, but no, sir.'

Ten days later Higgins wrote his first letter to Captain Price, and started a courtship which continued after marriage and for more than half a century. The couple seemed admirably suited to each other and an engagement was soon officially sanctioned by head-quarters.

The inevitable advisers urged the girl to wait a while, she was only 18. Her parents reasoned with her far into the night to show many reasons why she should not marry for a time. They pointed out the frailty of the Staff-Captain. Was he not a delicate man? 'He is so very thin. You'll be a widow within a year,' someone prophesied. There were too many Job's comforters. What should a young lass do?

She sought to know the will of God in this momentous matter and earnestly prayed for a sign. Accordingly she made up her mind that if more than 20 seekers came to the Penitent-form on a certain night she would accept Staff-Captain Higgins' proposal. Twenty-three people came forward.

The resulting engagement lasted 15 months, but since both the young people were chosen for special work, they found themselves stationed a considerable distance apart and saw little of each other. Staff-Captain Higgins was appointed divisional officer of the Oxford District of the Central Division and Captain Price proceeded to the command of the corps at Winchester.

About this time a new system for training cadets for officership was becoming established under the direction of Herbert Booth, the Founder's third son. Hitherto cadets had been trained only at the training home, Clapton. Now it was decided to divide their tuition between a period at Clapton and then in smaller groups of 15 to 20 at a number of provincial centres; and large houses were secured in nearly 30 towns and equipped for training purposes. Selected officers were appointed to command the local corps and to act as supervisors of training. Captain Price was appointed to this type of work and was made responsible for activities first in Winchester and later in Leighton Buzzard.

The training scheme—a learn-as-you-work project—provided for an instructional period at the centre during which the cadets were associated with the corps work of the town. This was followed by responsibility as cadet-officers and appointments, two by two, to village corps and new openings.

Skilled training officers with knowledge and experience were kept constantly on the move, visiting the centres for lectures and personal interviews, and clarifying problems met by the cadet-officers in their field work. This system provided a practical touch with the people and their needs and gave the opportunity of translating theories into practice. Another important consideration was that the scheme enabled a larger number of cadets to be prepared for officership than could be accommodated at Clapton.

In addition to divisional responsibilities Staff-Captain Higgins was given charge of training operations in Oxfordshire and Buckinghamshire. The work was exceedingly demanding, both physically and spiritually. The planning included countless details such as the securing of halls and quarters in the villages for the reception of each group of cadets as they left the Clapton Garrison for their field experience. By these methods in two years over 50 new societies were established in the two counties alone.

25

Travelling was by foot or by bicycle (the large wheel and small wheel, 'penny-farthing' model). In days when the telephone was a rarity and inexperienced cadet-officers made mistakes necessitating help or advice from divisional headquarters, it was not a case of a phone call to rectify matters, but a cycle trip. The divisional officer and his staff of six assistants in Oxford rarely ended their working days before midnight.

During the Staff-Captain's period of command in Oxford, in April 1887, he heard of disturbances in Buckingham, 25 miles away. Two young enthusiastic officers, Captain Anker Deans and Lieutenant Ralph Morris, had been summoned for 'unlawfully, in a certain street . . . called Nelson Street, sounding a certain musical instrument, to wit, a drum'.

This form of evangelism was not appreciated by the keeper of the Red Lion Inn, whose wife was ill. Although the drum-beating ceased when the fact was known, the officers, who refused to pay a fine of 42 shillings each, were sent to Aylesbury Jail for 14 days.

Staff-Captain Higgins supported his comrades in court and returned to the town a fortnight later to join Commandant Herbert Booth, Staff-Captain Harriet Lawrance and 3,000 people to welcome the prisoners home.

'They were happy days,' wrote Edward Higgins in retrospect. 'The fires of revival swept through many of those places and the glory of working for the salvation of souls helped to make bearable the demands of routine duties. Thousands of Salvationists were made. Corps were established, often in the crudest kind of meeting places; and officers, many of them to become leaders in the Movement, were born in the fervour of those days.'

Easter Monday, 2 April 1888, was the nuptial day, when Herbert Booth conducted the wedding of Catherine Price and Edward John Higgins, in the Corn Exchange, Oxford.

The crowds were greater than the available accommodation. As much as five shillings was offered for a seat. Five excursion trains were run to Oxford bringing thousands of people to the ceremony.

The actual marriage service was part of a day of evangelistic meetings. It was a simple wedding, no bridesmaids, no flowers, no best man. However, it was rich in glory, with many people kneeling at the Mercy Seat praying to the God of the bride and groom.

The bride could not have looked more radiant in the most expensive wedding gown. No couple could have been married in an atmosphere warmer with good wishes and comradely affection. Following the wedding luncheon, which was attended by many leading businessmen and friends of the Army in Oxford, the bridal pair slipped away for their brief honeymoon to Guernsey, in the Channel Islands.

The *Jackson's Journal* of 7 April 1888 reported the wedding thus:

The Salvation Army on Saturday, Sunday and Monday last, held great demonstrations in this city, their meetings taking place in the Corn Exchange, and the Household Troops Brass Band was brought in especially to take part in the proceedings. All services were attended so largely that numbers were unable to gain admittance.

The marriage of Staff-Captain Higgins and Captain Price was solemnized—'if one can use such a word in connection with the uproarious proceedings of The Salvation Army'—in the Corn Exchange at 11 o'clock on Easter Monday.

The building was crowded, both the floor, the galleries and the large platform; and the east end was filled with bandsmen and officers —men and women.

The bride and bridegroom were in the front row of the platform, the former in a blue uniform with a white sash and no adornment on the head; the latter in an undress blue uniform.

Upon the walls of the building were the following mottoes:

'Welcome to the Commandant'
'The World for Christ'
'God bless the union.'

Commandant Booth opened the proceedings with an extempore prayer, asking his hearers to pray not only for the bride and bridegroom, but for himself, 'for I feel a little bit nervous; I am only a young hand at this sort of thing'.

After the prayer came the hymns of the usual stirring character, interspersed by such ejaculations as:
'The sisters are laughing instead of singing.' 'Let's have that over again; I want to see those in the gallery sing like a Hallelujah musical box.'

A few verses of Scripture were read by Commandant Booth, who from the words 'Hear therefore and observe to do' drew a flattering contrast between the deeds of The Salvation Army and the theorizing of everybody else. This was his comment upon the verse, 'Take no thought what ye shall eat, or what ye shall drink'—'If we can't get a beefsteak we will get a turnip or a red herring. Let us thank God for what we do get.'

After an address of this character, lasting 20 minutes, another hymn was sung and then Commandant Booth came to the business of the meeting.

He told the people that the bridegroom had been six years on the roll of the Army and that he hoped they would all serve as long before getting married; that the bride had been a depot officer for three years, that they sought this marriage for the glory of God and the furtherance of the cause of The Salvation Army, that Captain Higgins loved Captain Price and, strange to say, Captain Price loved Captain Higgins. This evoked some laughter.

The Commandant went on to say that those who served in the Army must be married according to their Articles, which he then read out.

The marriage service was then proceeded with on the lines of the Church Service.

In the characteristic language of the day *The War Cry* also reported:

Easter Monday dawned bright and promising, filling every heart with gladness and expectation, and doubtless helping to crowd out our various excursion trains which ran from all parts of the district with huge freights of living, shouting, happy hearts. It was an imposing sight to see train after train arriving and load after load forming up into procession and marching off to the scene of action with bands playing and colours flying, and enthusiasm at white heat.

Unfortunately, some of the later arrivals had their enthusiasm severely tested on arrival at the hall by finding there was no room for them, but they 'kept believing' and enjoyed outside blessings since they could not have inside ones.

It is impossible to describe the boil and glory, the animation and fervour indoors, not only among the large numbers of new recruits but amongst the veteran soldiers and the staid, respectable outsiders who seemed quite to have got the salvation contagion, for that day, at any rate, and enjoyed themselves in orthodox salvation fashion.

The service throughout was listened to with intense interest and there was no doubt 'the popular DO' was properly united to his

28

popular bride, the pent-up feelings of that great crowd found vent in loud reverberations of praise and song and enthusiastic wishes of joy and blessing to the happy pair.

Then we betook ourselves to the Town Hall where the marriage banquet was spread and we listened to the district report read by the Commandant—a record of most marvellous advances.

Twelve months ago Staff-Captain Higgins was commissioned to take charge of the district. There were 19 corps and now there are 43, besides five others which have, in the course of the year, been given over to other districts.

When the Higgins returned from their honeymoon, Mrs Higgins found that all six assistants at the divisional headquarters, Oxford, were single young men who lived at the divisional officer's home. Therefore she had perforce to take them all under her care.

Marriage caused no slackening in the soul-saving quest of the Higgins. Singly, their passion had been to win souls for Christ; as a married team the primary object of their lives was the same. They were soon jointly absorbed in the care of the division and its officers. Meetings were held nearly every night. The week-ends provided full programmes often climaxed with an 'all night of prayer' on Monday. All this brought an unspeakable joy.

Within six months, however, they received marching orders and were appointed to the command of the West London District, which included the famous Regent Hall Corps. Here was privilege and opportunity greater than anything before, but Higgins was still not physically strong and the strain of divisional work proved too great. Even a position with less responsibility did not solve his health problem and he was given a year's sick furlough to be spent in Penarth with Mrs Higgins and their baby.

On recovery Higgins was appointed to be head of the Educational and Health Department of the Training Home in Clapton, to serve under Commissioner T. Henry Howard. In 1892 came promotion to the rank of Major and the following year appointment as second-in-command of training and corps work in the London area under Commissioner Evangeline Booth.

During these years London witnessed a work of great soul-saving power. In an open-air campaign at Highgate, for example, 32 men and women knelt at the drumhead one Sunday evening, the crowd being so great that traffic had to be stopped while they prayed for God's salvation.

At the funeral service of the Army Mother, held in Olympia on 13 October 1890, Major Higgins was one of the officers honoured to bear the casket.

In 1894 the Army's second international congress was held in London, an event which profoundly moved England, and in vivid and colourful fashion revealed something of the ever-growing activities of the Movement throughout the world. The Major had much to do with the congress planning and in the last officers' councils of the occasion, held at Clapton, the Founder promoted him to the rank of Colonel.

Two events in early 1896 made a great impression in the Higgins' family, now grown to three children, Edward (seven), Phillis (five) and Ernest (three).

After serving for six-and-a-half years at the training home, one Tuesday in April Colonel Higgins was summoned to the Founder's home at Hadley Wood. There he received marching orders to the United States to become the chief secretary (second in responsibility) of that great command. He was told an early departure was necessary, that there was no time for any protracted farewell meetings. It would be necessary for Mrs Higgins and the family to remain in London for the time being.

When the Colonel reached home that day his voice entered the house before him and loudly but calmly announced to the family, 'I'm going to America.'

Naturally the news was a great surprise to both Mrs Higgins and the children. The family also realized that he had shaved off his beard, an ornament he had worn since becoming a divisional officer.

Within four days, on 15 April 1896, Colonel Higgins sailed on the SS *Britannica* for New York, leaving his homeland for the first time.

6

Salvationism and service

ON 6 January 1896 Commander Ballington Booth, second son of the Founder, received marching orders to another appointment after a command of five years of the work in the United States. Eight other top leaders received similar orders at the same time. Ballington was persuaded to ask his father to allow him to stay, but William Booth, impartial leader that he was, insisted on loyalty from his children as from other officers.

As the days passed the leader in America felt he should stay in New York, and by March he had resigned from The Salvation Army and formed another evangelical movement, under his own direction, called the Volunteers of America.

This caused a split in the Army but, regrettable as this was, it was to prove to the world that the Army was bigger and stronger than any of its leaders.

William Booth appointed Commander Frederick St George de Lautour Booth-Tucker, with his wife, 'The Consul' (Emma, daughter of the Founder), as the new leaders for the United States, with Colonel Edward Higgins as their chief secretary (second-in-command).

The latter arrived in New York after a 10-day voyage. Unfortunately the machinery by which his time of arrival was to be made known had broken down and no one was at the quayside to meet him. Overlooking what might have seemed a cool welcome to a foreign country, the Colonel merely hailed a carriage and drove to the headquarters and announced his arrival. He was warmly received by the new leaders and sensed the internationalism of the Army spirit. A Britisher was welcomed to high leadership in America in a time of extreme crisis by Americans.

Higgins soon discovered perplexing problems facing the Army in the United States. The press appeared to be aligned against the new administration and many papers throughout the country mis-construed any action taken and presented even trivial happenings in the most unfavourable light. Ballington and Maud Booth were popular leaders enjoying the devotion of many of their officers; some were confused in their loyalties and joined the breakaway group. Others appeared uncertain, not knowing what course to take.

Obviously it was necessary for the new Commander and the Consul to make immediate contact with their forces on the widest possible front. Therefore, 11 days after Higgins' arrival, they set off to visit the land from coast to coast; and the new chief secretary left in New York was thrown upon his own resources.

Everything was new to the Englishman. He was surrounded by strangers. The methods and thinking of a new country had to be studied, then understood. Moreover, the absence of wife and family was a sore trial.

In this difficult time he learned to surrender utterly to God in prayer for both strength and guidance. He trusted the people around him, winning their esteem and confidence, and the result was a successful leader, quickly growing in capacity and maturity. In a situation demanding both skill in the management of affairs, as well as patience in the handling of men, he proved himself to be the man for the hour.

'Colonel Higgins could always be depended upon to give an officer a sympathetic, intelligent and fair hearing under all circumstances,' a colleague recalled years later. 'He never treated people as pegs but as personalities. That is what made him so approachable on the problems of ex-officers who sought re-acceptance after leaving the Army to follow the Ballington Booths. Realizing that many had been swept off their feet by the emotional force of a moment, he listened without prejudice to each applicant for reinstatement. When convinced of an officer's sincerity and basic loyalty to the Army, he was strong in his recommendations for re-acceptance. People felt that if Higgins knew the facts his decision would be speedy and fair.'

Higher in the scale of leadership Commander Booth-Tucker had a mind full of ideas, alive in initiative, with schemes that were daring and methods often unorthodox. The sound judgement and business acumen of his chief secretary became a sure anchor for Salvation Army policy which benefited greatly from the opposite and com-posite attributes of its top leadership.

Like inspired human whirlwinds, the Commander and the Consul toured the country at a pace which seemed impossible to maintain. Travelling by night to save time and spending the days in gatherings with officers and soldiers, they conducted public meetings in the evenings, a highly successful programme they then followed month after month. Confidence was restored and the Army regained in large measure the ground it had lost.

Back at National Headquarters Colonel Higgins kept the machinery functioning smoothly, proving himself a business genius in keeping up with the many new schemes which Booth-Tucker rapidly launched; and at every possible opportunity he was conducting soul-saving campaigns himself.

By the time Mrs Higgins arrived in the States, on 12 September 1896, her husband had imbibed a great deal of the American outlook, although the international ideal was indelible in all that he did. He was not yet a conversationalist after the American pattern, but still rather a shy man who thoroughly enjoyed listening. Nevertheless his alert responses and facial expressions always showed how thoroughly he entered into things and how keenly sensitive he was to all that happened around him. Little escaped his notice.

Great was the joy of the reunion, especially as there were now four children in the family, Wilfred having been born in England seven weeks previously. Husband and wife were once more a team.

With a vast territory to cover from the Atlantic to the Pacific, and with great responsibilities, the Colonel was seldom at home. Even three days after his wife had landed in New York he was speeding to Chicago for a pressing engagement. Such is the demanding schedule of an Army leader.

Absences notwithstanding, Edward Higgins was a great home man. His work came first, but he loved a 'rough and tumble' with the children. Mrs General Albert Orsborn (Phillis, the eldest daughter) has fond memories of rare but happy hours spent playing games with father. He was as anxious to take part in a game as any of the children, and very anxious to win too. He always played with vigour and enthusiasm. Both boys and girls liked it because he was not condescending in his attitude, being always keen, intelligent and a scrupulously fair antagonist. 'I was born into a happy home,' remembered Mrs Orsborn, his daughter, Phillis. 'I never knew it otherwise than happy, and although as the years went by there were shadows as come to most homes, there was never any discord. My father was saintly without being sanctimonious.'

In the Higgins' family the children loved their mother deeply. She was like a big sister to them all, but father was almost an object of worship. To go against his wishes made them feel mean and uncomfortable. They watched eagerly for his home-coming and vied with each other for the privilege of fetching his slippers.

In the home the Colonel had the happy facility of being able to lay aside the cares and problems of office as easily as washing a slate clean. He was loving and lovable, but not demonstrative, and family life moved along in a natural way, like a deep-flowing river unperturbed by storms and stress.

Official business was never discussed in the family circle. The children never heard their father complain. If official worries were greater and burdens came heavier, the elder ones knew of it only because they noticed that father was quieter than usual. Whatever his Army problems, or lack of them, he never lost his affectionate geniality and always gave an understanding ear to the youngsters' personal troubles and difficulties.

All members of the family were proud of father, of his rank, uniform and position in The Salvation Army. One daughter called him 'Colonel', even in the earliest years of her memory, and felt he was the most handsome man she knew.

'Father seldom administered physical punishment,' observed another daughter, 'but to feel any uncertainty concerning his attitude towards one's conduct was certainly punishment enough.' By the indirect method, unobtrusive but definite, he influenced the whole family.

The high point of these years from the children's standpoint was the brief vacation by the sea at Belmar, New Jersey, with its merry-go-round, ice-cream, a boat on Shark River, or a trolley-bus ride to Asbury Park. It was fun for all. Higgins played games with the boys and a victory over father at croquet was a great achievement. There were no tensions or barriers between father, mother and children in this family.

Ever a practical man, the Colonel carefully guided his boys and girls in a preparation of themselves for careers of usefulness. The

Higgins family never failed to be a happy one, whether there was one child or seven.

In spite of home responsibilities Mrs Higgins found opportunities, small and great, to be of service in Army work. The Consul soon realized her unusual aptitude and capacity to shoulder important duties, and recognized especially her wisdom and good judgement. She assumed the oversight of the New York Mercy Box Department and was later appointed the national secretary for women's social service and slum work. This responsibility entailed considerable travelling and in a few months Mrs Higgins had visited Boston, Chicago, Omaha, Grand Rapids, Cleveland, Philadelphia, San Francisco, and Portland, Oregon, in the interests of the women's work of the Army, covering thousands of miles in the trying railway journeys of that day.

There were eight homes and centres for women and children when Mrs Higgins entered office and she was able to see the number increased to 20 before handing over affairs to her successor. The Army's numerous institutions in the USA are built on the sound foundations which she laid.

America readily admits its debt to the Army, and Salvationists of the USA recognize their obligations to Edward Higgins, especially his part in the negotiations which led to the Act which provided for the incorporation of The Salvation Army. The Act became law on 28 April 1899, since when the Army has been recognized as a 'religious and charitable organization'.

For a number of years the Army was at a serious disadvantage in so far that under the laws of the various states it had no legal existence to aid its spiritual and social service work. This made it appear to lack soundness, security and enduring qualities.

For instance, the famous John D. Rockefeller contemplated donating $50,000 to the Army. He had been greatly impressed by an open-air meeting and, attending the subsequent indoor service, felt that here was a movement worthy of his generous support. Shrewd business man that he was, he decided he would first of all make due investigation of the Army and assigned the task to his secretary and to a brother-in-law. They examined the Army's system and methods and visited the New York Headquarters, where in an interview they suggested the advisability of incorporation. For some reason they were not encouraged and reported back to JDR who withheld his support. In later years, when incorporation had been effected, Mr Rockefeller contributed generously to the Army's cause.

During the Higgins' period in the States many building schemes were inaugurated and the property holdings greatly increased. In these and other plans his caution and far-sighted vision was linked to the high integrity and imagination of Booth-Tucker, the dauntless courage and enthusiasm of the Consul and the aggressiveness of four American leaders, unofficially spoken of as 'the big four'— Richard Holz (senior), Adam Gifford, William Evans and William McIntyre.

About this time, too, the successful holiness ministry of Samuel Logan Brengle, a young minister of great promise who had thrown in his lot with the Army, attracted the attention of Colonel Higgins. Ever keen to see the potential of a man, he recommended Brengle for appointment as national spiritual special—an office which brought him world influence and notice and eventually the Army's highest rank of Commissioner.

The living and preaching of the doctrine of holiness of heart is a cornerstone in the Salvation Army structure and Commissioner Brengle became one of the foremost exponents of the doctrine. All over the world his books on the subject are still in great demand and his name is everywhere revered by Salvationists.

During nine-and-a-half years' stay in America, Colonel Higgins undertook several important business journeys to the international centre in London, which strengthened his conviction of the vital nature of the Army's world-wide mission and the importance of its international spirit. But the strain and rush of those years took their toll.

In 1900 the Colonel, overworked and exhausted, finally found himself with a body which could no longer respond to the drive of his iron will. He suffered from a nervous breakdown with total incapacity for responsibility.

What a blow to an enthusiast whose very meat and drink was hard work! But he was wise to follow medical advice and four months later was able to report again for duty, physically a new man. He never looked back.

One day in October 1903, the Higgins' phone rang to announce the tragic death of the Consul. She was returning from a visit to Fort Amity, Colorado, one of the three farm colonies sponsored by her husband, Commander Booth-Tucker. With her secretary, Ensign Esther Dammes, and Colonel Thomas Holland she had boarded the night train for Chicago. Travelling between Kansas City and its destination, the train was wrecked during the following night, with the Consul fatally, and Colonel Holland seriously, injured. After the horrifying impact of the smash the Consul lived for only two hours, her promotion to Glory taking place from the roughly-built depot at Dean Lake, Missouri.

The blow to the Army was stunning; to the Commander irreparable. He had come from New York to meet her and only on arrival in Chicago did he learn of her death.

In heart-felt tribute Edward Higgins said: 'The influence and effect of the Consul's life during the seven-and-a-half years she laboured in the States, produced wonders in the minds of the American public. She took hold of the greatest men in the land and attached them as friends of the Movement. Her platform ability was of the highest order, swaying great audiences by her forceful and pungent arguments and by her sweet appeal. Her words turned many a crowd from hostility to sympathy. In council she had a master mind, seeing policies in the perspective of the immediate as well as the future. She managed men, difficult men, as few could do.'

In 1904 the Army's third international congress was held in London and the delegation from the United States was of considerable size. To the chief secretary's desk came the multitude of organizational plans concerning not only the transportation of 400 men and women, but details of councils, meetings and demonstrations in England. When the SS *Carpathia* sailed from New York on 14 July 1904, all the cabin accommodation was taken by Salvationists.

Colonel Higgins had planned a programme for almost every hour of the voyage, and the delegation that arrived at Liverpool was one of the happiest that ever sailed the seas. Two special trains carried the party to London, where almost immediately they were swallowed up by contingents from the rest of the world, ready to participate in one of the outstanding series of events in Salvation Army history.

7

International outlook

'REPORT at IHQ, London,' read marching orders received in 1905, and like good soldiers the Higgins saluted and reported. Thus ended a decade of happy service in their first overseas appointment.

After the 1904 congress, commissioner Evangeline Booth had been appointed to the American command, with Colonel William Peart as her chief secretary. She arrived in New York in 1905 and to Colonel Higgins fell the task of passing on the details of a great and growing organization; for these were years of virility and mobility for the Army in the United States, with young men advancing quickly to positions of leadership, fearless as adventurers for Christ and inspired by spiritual vision and unswerving devotion to the Army.

When Higgins returned to England, he was appointed assistant foreign secretary to Commissioner Booth-Tucker and later to Commissioner T. Henry Howard.

Here was a period of testing and readjustment. There was, for instance, the contrast between the comparative insignificance of the position in the Foreign Office and that of chief secretary in the United States. There were six children and it was difficult to find a quarters large enough within the rent allowance.

For Mrs Higgins the change was from days of overflowing activity and responsibility in the States to having little to do, in a public sense, outside the usual programme of the nearby corps. Nevertheless new horizons soon began to show themselves and with them an international parish.

In his new position Higgins became a well-known figure in all the European countries. He travelled extensively with the Founder and Bramwell Booth and was frequently one of a small company called to conferences at William Booth's home.

The Army was speeding its march round the world and Colonel

Higgins handled much of the financial and other details attendant on the rapidly expanding work. Especially was he responsible for the development of many missionary enterprises.

Moreover, since Commissioner Booth-Tucker was a great spiritual force, conducting remarkable campaigns in which Higgins had often been his chief assistant, the younger man became fired with a zeal for international evangelism.

The Army's Founder liked Higgins' reading voice and it was a delight for the young Colonel to read to his General for hours between engagements. These were days of privilege in which he imbibed still more of what is demanded and involved in front-rank Army leadership.

Among his campaigns with William Booth were those in 1907 and two years later that in Russia. He never forgot the Swedish Congress held in Stockholm, when a fleet of steamers was chartered to bring 12,000 Salvationists to the meetings.

Among the staff of the Foreign Office Higgins became greatly loved. When he heard of the delay in remittances reaching missionary lands and the inconvenience caused to certain officers, he spared no effort until the matter was righted. He was kindly disposed to the wives of his staff and considered them in assignments that had to be made. Often he would say to his secretary, 'Get home to your wife. I may be late but you needn't wait for me.'

While campaigning in France in 1907 the Colonel received an urgent call from his father, Commissioner Higgins, then in charge of Scotland. At once he turned homewards, but the elder man had been promoted to Glory before he arrived at his side. It was a great blow, for a close comradeship existed between father and son, the former always being tremendously fond of 'Ted' and proud of his place in Army affairs.

The elder Higgins was one of the lesser-known but grand characters of the Army whose service in London, India and Scotland, and in charge of the Subscribers' Department at International Headquarters, was rich in great accomplishments for God. A tall, stately, picturesque and inspiring figure, he had a long flowing beard, flashing eyes, sonorous voice. He was eloquent of speech and full of whimsical humour.

Conscientious to a scruple, Commissioner Higgins annoyed the cashiers at headquarters by his insistence in settling his petty cash account daily instead of weekly. When he died in Glasgow his memorandum book of expenses was balanced up to the previous night, and on a nearby table was a stack of letters written in his own hand, answering those of the previous day. Even his clothes were laid out neatly for the morrow.

Bramwell Booth conducted the impressive funeral service in Glasgow, but the burial was in Abney Park Cemetery, London, near a spot later to be hallowed by the mortal remains of his beloved Founder.

After six years of service in the Foreign Office, Colonel Higgins was promoted in rank and appointed British Commissioner, with the direction of all field activities in the United Kingdom.

He received his orders direct from William Booth, in the Founder's room at Hadley Wood. Together the two men knelt in prayer, with the octogenarian praying for the younger, invoking God's blessing on him and strength and wisdom for his great task.

Edward Higgins
as Chief Secretary
in the
United States
of America

Mrs General Higgins

8

In the Spirit of the Lord

FROM *War Cry* reports, the installation of Commissioner Higgins as British Commissioner by the Chief of the Staff, Bramwell Booth, in the Regent Hall, London, was a brilliant occasion. The famous 'Rink' was crowded; the gathering was notable for its happiness, music, prayer and inspiration, and since everyone knew that the new leader of the British Territory was a Salvationist from 'tip to toe', there were pledges of loyalty and words of eulogy that might easily have turned the head of a lesser man.

Not so with Edward Higgins. At the end of the meeting he was not found in the glare of the spotlight or receiving the congratulations of friends. He was kneeling with a broken-hearted man at the Penitent-form.

The incident makes it easy to consider the progress of everything preceding it in due perspective. There was the terse, typical message from the Founder which read: 'Tell Higgins to do his duty'; and a generous tribute from Bramwell Booth in which he declared: 'I believe that my dear brother and comrade, who has been serving under my direction for many years, can confidently invite you to follow him as he follows Christ. He is worthy of your confidence and affection, and in the General's name I have great pleasure in presenting him to you. He will not fail you in example, in love, in patience, and in suffering, if needs be. Take him to your hearts and trust him.'

Climaxing the oratory of the evening, the new Commissioner said in words typical of his deep affection for the Army and its leaders: 'I love the Army better than anything in this wide world and I believe in it with all my heart . . .!' Then at the end of an impassioned address, he quoted an incident from the Duke of Wellington's life: 'Give me one grip of your all-conquering hand and I'll do it,' said a general on receiving one of the Iron Duke's difficult commands. He received his request, and he did his job.

'I have the grip of my General in this great undertaking,' declared

41

the Commissioner, 'and I value it beyond words; but best of all, I have the grip of the all-conquering hand of my blessed Lord and Master—whose I am and whom I serve. My eyes are up to Him and at His word I march forward.'

By councils, rallies, meetings and demonstrations, Commissioner and Mrs Higgins were welcomed as the leaders of the British Territory in the larger towns of the British Isles. In a demonstration of the Army's strength in Wales, 30 bands were included in a massed welcome meeting at Cardiff.

As British Commissioner, Edward Higgins could view Salvation Army history as successive periods of revival years: a consolidation era; the period for organization; and the time for discipline, evolving into a period of strict and strong controls. Some of the latter, administered sometimes with mistaken zeal, might easily have ushered in a period of retrogression for the Army, for not a few officers, feeling fettered and hobbled by systems and directives, were discouraged sometimes to the point of giving up the fight.

On becoming British Commissioner, Higgins made five resolves: to dedicate himself to a revival of religion; to develop the Army's youth work; to give Salvationists a clearer understanding of their responsibility for the salvation of the world; to realize the great responsibility of the field officer; and to understand that the future of the Army pivots on the zeal of its officers. He drew up his programme accordingly.

Comparatively young and endowed with keen insight and enthusiasm, he brought an invigorating atmosphere of progress and advance. Virtually living on the field, he went around the territory like a fire. Tireless in energy and ever in the forefront of a holy crusade, he travelled unceasingly, sleeping on trains and sometimes in stations between engagements. He soon achieved the reputation as an indefatigable worker and a hard hitter.

His forces were stirred to tremendous Kingdom-extending efforts. New projects were launched. The Army in Britain quickened its step. Great victories in memorable spiritual campaigns are on record. Advance was the order of the day; victory the news of the hour.

He early won the loyalty and co-operation of his officers. His fairness and justice were apparent to all and these qualities could be depended upon in his administration. As a leader he was big enough to reverse a decision if new facts proved a former judgement to be wrong.

No one ever heard him speak disparagingly of a comrade. That may have been in part because he was a quiet, strong man, not given to confidences; but beyond that he never failed to be conscious of the dignity of the individual and his interest in all officers as persons was keen and sympathetic. It was an unfailing rule that he be informed immediately of any sorrow or other serious trouble in an officer's life. Inevitably he made an officer's sorrow or trouble his own, and when he wrote it was generally in his own hand.

A prodigious writer of personal notes to officers and soldiers on a variety of matters, he mailed postcards by the thousand. Each carried a message from his heart. Hard times, sickness, bereavement, discouragement, success and good striving were never overlooked. If his train stopped at a station it was a reminder of the officers toiling in that town, and out would come pen and postcard. Soon a brief but personal message would be on its way to bring encouragement, often like a ray of sunshine, announcing the brightest dawn, to the officer on the receiving end.

When he heard of a young woman Captain having a difficult time at her corps he offered his help. She could hardly believe her eyes as she read the letter. Hers was such a hard struggle which was emphasized by the ignorance of the townspeople concerning the Army, its aims and work. But here was a Heaven-sent opportunity to enlighten them. She arranged a public meeting in the town hall with the mayor presiding. The hall was packed for the occasion. A great impression for good was made by the Commissioner and in consequence of it all the Captain's job became considerably easier.

Salvationists felt that here was a man unafraid of difficulties, one who would always approach a problem realistically, with an anxiety to be fair, just and kind. It seemed that while he dealt with matters with balanced judgement as they affected the present, his eye was ever on the future of the man or the problem and he made his decisions accordingly.

The 'BC', as he was unofficially called, was ever looking for young men and women of promise and did not fail to give them responsibilities which would bring out the very best in their character, mind and ministry. He was extraordinarily alert to the needs of the day and had a clever faculty of finding the right person for the job in hand.

In the same way that he found many other leaders he discovered Albert Orsborn, then a young Captain commanding a small corps. The British Commissioner visited the division to discuss personnel needs and Orsborn's name was mentioned in connection with the requirements of a much larger corps. The fact of the Captain's youth was quickly brushed aside.

'Does he tackle his own difficulties?' he asked. When he received an affirmative answer, he ordered: 'Put him in.'

Thus came the moment of opportunity for the junior officer who in future years would follow in his own footsteps to become the Army's sixth General.

Every item of Commissioner Higgins' meetings focused on the supreme object of calling for decisions for Christ. In a holiness meeting he was not satisfied unless the Mercy Seat was lined with men and women kneeling and praying for power to live a holy life. In a salvation meeting everything was planned to lead to the Penitent-form. 'Decide for Christ; decide now; make your decision an open confession,' was his constant clarion call.

Whether the meeting consisted of an audience of 50 or thousands, it made no difference; he gave his zealous, wholehearted, impassioned best. The small corps ranked equally with the large one as objects of his intense love and effort. He proved himself a deft painter of word pictures and in his platform utterances never failed by language and gesture to make Bible characters live.

A standing rebuke to the dawdler, the shuffler, the muddler and the man always behind time, Edward Higgins' motto was 'Be in time'. He missed only one train in his life, an American sleeper, and that was wrecked and almost every person on board was killed or seriously injured. On this occasion he regarded the miss as divine interference on his behalf, although losing this train caused him great annoyance at the time.

The Commissioner did not particularly want to be seen off at railway stations or to be met on arrival for engagements. 'I want no man to carry my bag,' he said so many times. He was a humble man.

The famous initials E.J.H. always stood for a charming guest. He never took for granted a kindness or courtesy. His smile was infectious.

On one occasion he was entertained at a home in Belfast where an aged mother lived with her daughter, his hostess. When he had gone, the mother said to her daughter, 'What a beautiful face he has!' Later, he was again in Belfast and learning the mother was ill called upon her. When about to leave he prayed with her and then, holding her frail hand, leaned down and kissed her cheek, no doubt remembering his own beloved mother. Then he tenderly bade her farewell, with a fervent 'God bless you, mother!'

According to some of his associates, The Salvation Army in Britain seldom boasted a better businessman of such rare executive ability as Edward Higgins. He had outstanding perception, capacity and ability in this direction. In a business conference he invariably made notes and asked that others should do the same. These he insisted on seeing. Corrections were made and the resulting agreement initialled so that no disputes or misunderstandings were possible. He kept a meticulous record of transactions.

When he presided at business talks he demanded all the facts and never made decisions in a hurry. A matter was not finalized until his mind was absolutely satisfied.

But Higgins' outstanding executive skills did not prevent him from being a successful evangelist. No matter how tiring the business burdens of a day, he invariably came to the public platform at night radiant, wholly renewed and rarely seemed to tire.

Shortly after taking office as British Commissioner, Edward Higgins launched the Siege of London. While the actual concentrated period was from 2 to 11 November, it was preceded by four months of prayer by way of preparation.

A London newspaper-man described the effort as 'a colossal piece of cheek', but by its spiritual implications it could hardly be dismissed so easily. In the Metropolitan Police area the co-operation of 10,000 Salvationists was enlisted for special spiritual service in addition to their customary Salvation Army duties. So this great host of volunteer crusaders went out on missions of personal evangelism, to visit people in their homes, to take the gospel to the public-houses, to hunt up backsliders with special invitations to the meetings, to speak with people on the streets concerning the claims of Christ and to bring to the Army halls as many non-church-going people as possible.

For 10 days something extraordinary took place simultaneously at the 150 London corps. On two Saturday nights, for instance, every public-house in the district was visited with the gospel message and, as far as possible, every habitué was spoken to personally about his soul's salvation.

Special open-air meetings were arranged late at night to meet the crowds coming from the places of amusement and out of the 'pubs'. Workers were on duty all day at 'Siege' centres to give advice on matters spiritual. At all times of the day neighbourhood prayer meetings were held in the homes of the people, and in London's City Temple. Salvationists met to pray during their lunch hour.

'We go for all and we go for the worst. We go in desperation,' was the slogan and spirit of London Salvationists as they advertised their meetings with colourful sandwich-board parades and raids into the city's worst and most notorious dens of iniquity.

Said the British Commissioner, with an infectious enthusiasm, as early in the campaign he was in the van of activities: 'Talk to people everywhere—of Jesus . . . get your neighbours interested . . . sing the songs of salvation and get everybody else to sing them . . . pray not only silently and in secret, but burst out in prayer when opportunity presents itself.' He gave 17 addresses in a week.

The results of the Siege were amazing. During the 10 days 10,000 people knelt at the Mercy Seat, including many 'trophies of grace'. There was 'Cheeky Charlie' of Hammersmith, typical of many jail-birds, and a woman who had been in prison 20 times and more. At Penge 99 captures were made at that corps alone, and in Soho the worst drunkard of the district was saved. Norland Castle rejoiced greatly in many converts as notorious as those miracles of grace described by Harold Begbie in his *Broken Earthenware*.

Following a drunkards' raid, a woman came to the Army hall. She was in a dirty condition and had two black eyes. That night she became converted and soon became an evangelist of the printed word, visiting the public-houses with copies of *The War Cry*. Her home, terribly neglected and in a dreadful state at the time of her conversion, became entirely changed. Her husband came to the meetings and found Christ as Saviour for himself.

As a result of the Siege at another corps over 40 converts were made into soldiers, some of them eventually becoming officers.

One day a man with murder in his heart against another who had led his wife into unfaithfulness was passing the City Temple doors. He saw the Army folk entering and not knowing quite why, he followed them in. In his pocket was a revolver; in his burning brain were plans to use it, first to murder his enemy, then to kill himself.

As the meeting progressed, he sat still with a great pain in his heart. By song and word there came to him the message, 'My grace is sufficient for thee', and he was deeply moved. At the close of the gathering he sought the officer in charge and, not without a struggle, became a new man in Christ Jesus.

The Siege kindled a great spiritual hunger and a new spirit of enthusiasm for aggressive Christianity. Battle reports came to the British Commissioner each night and a summary of them was daily relayed to the corps officers.

In London more than 1,000 new senior soldiers were enrolled from the Siege effort, over 400 of them being sworn-in by the British Commissioner at Camberwell.

Many important and historically moving events of Salvation Army history took place during Edward Higgins' command of the British Territory. Rarely has a more emotionally stirring epic happened to any organization than the promotion to Glory of the Founder, General William Booth, on Tuesday 20 August 1912. When God's soldier laid down his sword to take up the crown, the world stood to attention in honouring salute. Salvationists of the nations grieved because of the passing of the first Salvationist, yet rejoiced because heavenly hosts had welcomed a valiant warrior to his eternal reward.

Merely to look through the brochure giving the order of the funeral and memorial services is to sense again the deep emotions of the 35,000 people who crowded Olympia, London, for the memorial service on 28 August. Tens of thousands paid their tribute to a great friend as the procession of 10,000 Salvationists, five miles long, made its way in solemn pageant to Abney Park Cemetery on the following day.

The Olympia service was conducted by the aid of numbered cards which coincided with numbers on the very detailed programme. So we read: (1) The United Bands, consisting of the International Staff Band and the Chalk Farm, Regent Hall and Tottenham Corps Bands, will play a verse of the tune 'Better World' once through. Then (2) All are requested to rise and sing the following verses. Here followed three verses of 'There is a better world, they say'.

As the 'Dead March in *Saul*' was being played, the funeral procession with its 26 sections entered. We also read that 'Commissioner Lawley will pray'; that we should stand and sing, or sit and sing, or follow a Scripture reading led by Commissioner Higgins, or read in silence words of the Founder. Then came the page appealing for surrenders. Page 29 calls the unconverted to 'Rise to your feet now! and make your way to the Mercy Seat provided on the right and left of the platform. Officers are there to help you. Come and kneel close beside the casket containing the remains of one who spent his life in trying to win you. Come while we all sing.' And so on, through the moving moments of a deeply impressive Covenant Service to the final song: 'When the roll is called up yonder, I'll be there!'

The thought and care in preparation of such a programme enables it to glow with inspiration in spite of the years.

Over 50 brigades, including 39 bands, made up the impressive funeral procession which marched from the International Headquarters, Queen Victoria Street, to Abney Park Cemetery. The nations of the world were represented. At the Mansion House the acting lord mayor waited in salute. London's traffic stopped for more than three hours. The busiest city in the world paid homage to a simple servant of Jesus Christ, one of her illustrious freemen. Nearly 3,000 police were on duty. London wrote the amazing epic indelibly into her record.

At the graveside the great throng sang: 'My Jesus, I love Thee.' General Bramwell Booth brought the deeply stirring eulogy of a son and successor. Evangeline Booth paid her tribute, first in silent weeping with the sorrowing crowd, then in tender phrases which belong only to her. Mrs Commissioner Lucy Booth-Hellberg, the Founder's youngest daughter, too overcome to sing as a solo, 'There is a fountain filled with Blood', spoke instead.

For the British Territory, Commissioner Higgins said in part: 'All through the centuries the name of the Army's hero will be remembered with reverence and gratitude. . . . Our tribute is one of eternal devotion to the principles for which his life was spent. . . .

He was against all sham and hypocrisies. So we will be. He stood for that which was true and noble and pure. So will we.'

Then the final song of the funeral service with the chorus:

> *No retreating, hell defeating,*
> *Shoulder to shoulder we stand;*
> *God, look down, with glory crown*
> *Our conqering band.*
> *Victory for me*
> *Through the Blood of Christ, my Saviour;*
> *Victory for me*
> *Through the precious Blood.*

Surely to have participated in such proceedings was to sense the spirit of salvationism in a time of testing, and to hear the heartbeat of the Army, vigorous and spiritually strong.

A hundred thousand people had paid tribute to William Booth during a four-days' lying-in-state at the Clapton Congress Hall. When distributing the Founder's meagre personal effects, Bramwell Booth sent Higgins a silk handkerchief—a prized keepsake.

Another important event of this period was the international congress of 1914.

The magnitude of organizational detail can be realized from the fact that some 2,000 delegates, speaking 34 languages, were in London for more than 100 meetings spread over the two weeks and more which made up the congress period. The welcome and farewell meetings were held in the Royal Albert Hall, crowded to capacity three times in those weeks. A Hyde Park demonstration, featuring a procession from the London Embankment, saw 12,000 Salvationists parade. Attendances at meetings numbered approximately 1,250,000. General and Mrs Bramwell Booth and certain delegates were received by the royal family, the Prime Minister and the Archbishop of Canterbury.

At a great Crystal Palace Thanksgiving Day there were 200 bands and a march past of 40,000 which, five miles long, took one-and-a-half hours to pass the saluting base.

Fifty thousand people thronged the Crystal Palace grounds at 8.30 am and increased during the day to the largest crowd 'this glorified conservatory of Sir Joseph Paxton' had ever held. It was an event of great colour, indescribable enthusiasm and memorable blessings. At the close of the day Commissioner Higgins prayed: 'We have been through the hours of this day crowning Thee our King. . . . From this beautiful day may there spread an influence for God and righteousness which shall not cease until tens of thousands, hundreds of thousands, have been brought to Jesus.'

The *Daily Chronicle* reported that 'not one visitor could have left the big glass palace without feeling a thrill of joy that there was so much happiness in the world'.

Newspapers described the congress as 'a great triumph', 'a welter of delight'. Said one commentator: 'The Army has proved that it stands on its own feet, a God-created and a God-preserved movement.'

Nations shared in a myriad emotions, thoughts and ideas common to them all. All were knit in sympathy as they shared Canada's sorrow in the loss of so many of her delegates by the sinking of the *Empress of Ireland*.

For all who participated in such a congress there were experiences linked with the eternities; and for all concerned in its direction, epics of leadership demanding and important.

These were also the days when two new Salvation Army youth sections—the life-saving scouts (for boys) and the life-saving guards (for girls)—were inaugurated as important parts of Commissioner Higgins' programme for youth.

On 21 July 1913 in the Clapton Congress Hall was the introduction of the Army's first scout troop (Chalk Farm), which paraded with Robert James as its commissioned leader. Major (later Commissioner) Hugh Sladen was appointed the territorial organizer and General Bramwell Booth became the first president.

Within a few months thousands of boys were enrolled and by the time of the organization's first united appearance in public at the Crystal Palace, on 23 June 1914, there were 65 units. Major Sladen headed a large contingent of scouts in a Hyde Park march, a spectacular event during the international congress.

On 17 November 1915 the life-saving guard (later guides) movement was launched by Mrs General Booth at the Regent Hall,

London, with Major (later Lieut.-Colonel) Margaret Fitzgerald as the territorial organizer. Commissioner Higgins was commander-in-chief.

The Commissioner listened to Guard Burgess, of Nunhead, recite the guard declaration and was to say 'Amen!' to the sentiments. The words 'pleasant under all circumstances'—often later used as a code word PUAC—especially found an echo in his heart.

Throughout his life he was able to do difficult and hard things with a smile—a smiling leader who looked pleasant not because of a disregard of the tests of the battle, but because of the righteousness of his cause and the certainty of victory.

With this kind of smile early in 1913 he had announced two ambitious plans: to open 50 new corps simultaneously on a Sunday toward the end of May, and to release 100 officers from the British field for missionary service, chiefly in India. Both projects were successful.

Because of his love for missionary lands, Commissioner Higgins shared the thrill of thousands as the Memorial Missionary Party of 102, with the gleaming cross in full view, heard the General's solemn charge to them at the Royal Albert Hall. Gay and colourful in the costumes of missionary countries, they marched through the City of London creating a profound impression. Five thousand people attended the final farewell meeting from the Sun Hall, Liverpool, on Monday 23 June. Up to that time this was the largest Salvation Army missionary party to leave England's shores. They left a trail of inspiration for many more young people to follow; follow they did, and follow they do.

Emphasizing the importance of youth evangelism, the Commissioner planned an 18-months' long 'Young Life Crusade'. This was launched in June 1913 with four days of councils with young people's local officers at Blackpool and Southsea, with 400 attending at each centre. Among the many objectives decided upon were 100 more young people's singing companies and 50 additional young people's bands. Edward Higgins may not have majored in music at school, but he never failed to emphasize its importance as a leader.

A typical Higgins' act was seen in November 1911, when he visited Hastings to welcome home from prison Mrs Adjutant Walter French and Ellen Parks and Kitty Jackson, with Bandsman Henry

Lee—four Salvationists who had served 14 days in Lewes jail for preaching the gospel. For the first nine days they had had only the 'hard labour' fare of 'skilly' and hard bread. After that they had been allowed cocoa. These suffering Salvationists needed support and their top leader gave them all the encouragement he could.

Hastings presented a challenging situation. The local magistrates had already issued many summonses for no just reason at all. No evidence of destruction or disorder was submitted by the police. For years Salvationists had held their meetings on the spot in question. Suddenly their freedom to preach the gospel was questioned and threatened, and like true people they were prepared to fight and suffer for their liberty and rights.

By a Home Office order benefits could be given 'to persons whose conduct included no moral turpitude', but these were never applied to Salvationists. Ten 'Army people' went to jail and served an aggregate of 133 days. Heavy fines were inflicted. Some were paid by well-wishers but always against the wish of those on whom they were inflicted.

Eventually Hastings Salvationists won their fight and today they continue to enjoy their freedom.

Ever practical, and particularly in times of crisis, the British Commissioner met his divisional commanders immediately after the outbreak of the First World War and planned emergency work to become as famous and familiar as the Army's red jerseys and poke bonnets.

Among servicemen Salvationists already had a chain of naval and military homes. These were at once placed at the disposal of the government. Rest and food centres were also set up in buildings handed over to Salvationists in Kensington, as well as a 600-bed hostel in Westminster. In Belgium a similar building with capacity for 100 men was filled nightly.

Early in the war, Salvation Army rest and refreshment tents were erected in (or near) most military camps. Greatly appreciated by the military authorities, these were ordered to be moved as part of the military equipment in times of transfer. In due course the tents were replaced by huts.

Salvation Army ambulances supplied a great need, not only for the speedy transport of the wounded from battlefield to base, but for a spiritual ministry to the badly maimed and dying. Over 50,000 wounded were conveyed by the first ambulance unit alone. When inspecting this and other work in France, Commissioner Higgins was greatly impressed by the splendid reputation Salvationists had made. The brass band of 24 members had added not only a 'touch of home' for the ambulance workers, but served to bring cheer in the midst of depression.

The Commissioner also proposed the setting up of motor kitchens or travelling refreshment rooms. Officers were set aside for military camp work and became important factors in morale building as they gave advice, wrote letters, organized games and made home contacts with wives and families for men with away-from-home problems.

Directed by Mrs Commissioner Higgins, the women of the home league provided comforts and parcels for the troops, as well as clothing for refugees.

Air-raid relief was added to the corps officers' responsibility; war widows were visited, assisted and comforted; the horrifying Silvertown explosion of 1917 found the Army's disaster relief activities functioning superbly; and a flag day was held.

The Army's post-First World War activities developed as red shield hostels and canteens appeared, often as by a miracle, on the heels of the British and American armies of occupation. When the troops recognized the Salvation Army flag flying from the roof of a house it meant a thrill for hundreds of thousands who were not Salvationists as well as for those who were.

Following days of war Commissioner Higgins was awarded the CBE (Commander of the Order of the British Empire) in recognition of his direction of the Army's humanitarian activities.

'Trust not in bricks and mortar' was an aphorism often heard in the British Commissioner's officers' councils. He believed rather in investing in people. At the same time, as a realist, he knew the value of adequate buildings to house the Army's many-sided activities.

Thus between 1912 and 1919 many building schemes were launched for the erection of corps halls and other centres of Army activity. The stone-laying and opening of such buildings became days to remember as, for example, when Prince Henry of Battenberg laid

53

the foundation stone for the Portsmouth naval and military centre, with the Marquis of Winchester presiding.

Today, one of the world's largest movements for women can be found within the organization of the Army in its home league—an international sisterhood united to raise and maintain the standards of home and home-making. To Mrs Higgins fell an honoured part in its pioneering.

On Monday 28 January 1907, the home league was inaugurated by Mrs General Bramwell Booth in the Cambridge Heath Hall, London, and the first local branch came into being immediately afterwards at Leytonstone, an East London corps, with Mrs Colonel Higgins as the first home league secretary. From the first meeting, with 16 women attending, she found herself a central figure.

Years later, as the wife of the British Commissioner and as territorial home league president, she was the inspiration of more than 1,000 home leagues in the British Isles, where annual rallies of women would number one or two thousand at each centre.

Ever an advocate of total abstinence the British Commissioner was a lover of the drunkard even as he hated the cause of his downfall. Periods were set aside, usually of a week's duration, when special efforts were made in a threefold direction: to save the drunkard; to warn the young of the folly and sin of drunkenness; and to bring about the Sunday closing of public-houses to give publicans and their employees the physical and spiritual benefits of God's sabbath. To help in the third objective he sent a personal letter to every publican in England.

What has been written in this chapter is but a sample of the success God granted to the Somerset lad who rose to the command of the Army's evangelical forces in the land of its birth.

9

Growing greatness

WHEN Commissioner T. Henry Howard retired from active service in 1919, General Bramwell Booth chose Commissioner Higgins as his Chief of the Staff.

It was not a position Higgins would have chosen and he accepted the will of his leader with something approaching apprehension. For in the new sphere he knew that much of his love for the public platform would have to be subordinated to working and planning behind the scenes. A great deal of time formerly spent in travelling the roads would be devoted to building pathways along which others might travel. In a sense, too, he would have to be the lieutenant rather than the commander.

Nevertheless the very character of the man called for an uttermost surrender to the new task with all that was his in hand, heart, mind and soul.

Much had to be learned. The acquaintance he had so far gained with phases of Army warfare had carried him only to the periphery of the inner circle of Salvation Army planning. Wisely he set himself to acquire the new and intrinsic knowledge belonging to the very centre of world-wide administration. There was the social service work with its network of problems, and legal arrangements and property affairs in many lands, financial principles and systems, both those affecting the raising and custody of money, as well as those regulating the expenditure. Each of these subjects might well have engrossed the total attention of an ordinary man. But the Chief of the Staff became equal to the task. He met the demands of his high office in a way that commanded the respect of all.

For 10 years Edward Higgins was the man who carried out Bramwell Booth's great schemes for the Army. This he did with admirable loyalty, thoroughness and buoyancy of spirit. He was rarely in the spotlight, sometimes 'on the spot', but he met his problems with both courage and sincerity.

There grew a great bond of affection between the General and his Chief, a bond revealed in one of the first communications to reach General Bramwell Booth on his birthday in 1919. It was a typical Higgins' letter of well-wishing in which he wrote among other things:

> It is a joy to serve you, and I am specially favoured to be brought into such close relationships with one whom, all my life practically, I have honoured and loved. . . . Each passing year has increased my admiration and deepened my affection for you.

At all important Salvation Army occasions which marked the years 1919–29, the figure of the Chief of the Staff was at the right hand of his General, with kindly countenance, dynamic word, shrewd direction. Higgins was a man clothed with efficiency and sound judgement. 'An immense strength to the Army fabric,' was a reporter's evaluation of the Movement's second man at the 1922 International Headquarters' councils.

In the trying times of 1928 he ever sought to give credit where credit was due. Speaking at a conference with life-saving scout and guard leaders at Clapton, he said: 'Perhaps you young people do not realize today how much you owe to the General. He it was who blazed the trail, fighting against opposition and overcoming almost insurmountable difficulties in order that the Army might lead the way in work amongst the young people.'

Edward Higgins' record as Chief of the Staff shows him exemplary in his selflessness. 'To serve God and the Army' was the dominant passion of his living. He was prepared to play 'second fiddle' (and what a delightful part he made of it) if it served the interests of his General and the Kingdom of God. He was ever prepared to risk misunderstanding and to endure hurt without a murmur, if only God was glorified and the Army was helped.

There were occasions, of course, when he was not in agreement with Bramwell Booth's policies, but that did not make him less loyal to his leader. At such times he was frank in stating his opinions, but they never interfered with his ardour in carrying out the General's wishes.

Throughout the early difficult days of the first High Council that affection remained deep and sincere.

In a tribute to Bramwell Booth after he had succeeded him as General, Edward Higgins declared in part:

His character needs no protection, for the Army everywhere speaks of its strength and beauty, and no shadow caused by passing misunderstandings ever remained long enough to dim its loveliness, but from all such experiences it emerged in greater contrast to all that was weak and ignoble.

His life's work needs no protection. It stands and speaks for him, and whilst time lasts will still stand, for those specific things for which Bramwell Booth will particularly be remembered, which have become such firm and necessary institutions as to make them more than likely to remain a part of our structure as long as any part of our building stands.

I think the mistakes Bramwell Booth made were remarkably few when one considers the tremendous and numerous decisions that rested in his hands. That he did make some, no one would have been more free to acknowledge than he, and we should only spoil a beautiful picture of a triumphant life if we tried to visualize him as somebody untouched by human infirmities. No, he was a man, but a great man; a statesman; a maker of men; a leader whose exploits in the world of social science and religious effort will be remembered with gratitude by us all and by those who will follow us.

Few men had the calm and collected poise of the Chief of the Staff. Arriving in New York for an American campaign in 1920, he found himself one night on a famous Cunarder which was safely berthed without the passengers being allowed to disembark. 'A considerable Salvation Army contingent was on hand to welcome the Chief of the Staff,' wrote Fritz Nelson. 'But alas, it was late in the evening and the announcement was made that no one could land until the following day.

'The news caused considerable chagrin among the welcoming Salvationists on the quayside. I was the only Salvationist allowed on board. Most of the passengers were in a state of annoyance and excitement. But not Commissioner Higgins; he was found in a quiet spot in one of the public rooms, finishing an interesting book.

'Meanwhile the Salvationists had gone to some lengths to discover ways and means which might enable their leader to land that night, but without success. Things had reached an impasse and the delegation of welcomers was standing in doleful silence when the Commissioner came to the ship's rail with that famous smile and a twinkle in his warm brown eyes. He looked down upon the frustrated group, waved his hand in greeting and told them to go home and get to bed. "As for myself," he said, "I'm going to do the same and I'll be seeing you all tomorrow." He had an inner calm which enabled them to be completely at ease.'

Edward Higgins never allowed the business cares of his office to outweigh his soul-saving zeal. In large meetings or small, his delight was to lead people to Christ. After a remarkable meeting in the Glasgow City Hall, when nearly 200 people knelt at the Mercy Seat, he exclaimed to Colonel (later Commissioner) George Langdon: 'This has been one of the greatest days of my life!'

Yet he was as anxious over one seeker as over many. Langdon remembers a meeting in Peterhead. A large crowd filled the building, but when the invitation to seek Christ was given, the audience rose as a man and made for the exits. But one man hesitated: and he became the convert of the evening. The Chief hovered over him, praying for his salvation, seemingly undisturbed by a turn of events which must have been disappointing.

With whatever phase of Army work he was dealing, Edward Higgins always yearned for the salvation of men. To the International Social Council, in 1921, he said:

Our purpose is not charity merely, nor ameliorative effort merely; neither is it penal. Ours is a work of redemption—of regeneration.

To tide a man over a difficulty is one thing; to put him in a position to master his besetment or difficulty is another.

To deal with the consequences of wrong and temporarily to alleviate its resultant suffering is one thing; to deal with the wrong itself, to remove the cause of the suffering, and exercise a loving care that makes it easier for the sufferer to do right, is quite another.

Our work is character building—often the rebuilding of it.

10

Toward the first High Council

NO story concerning Edward Higgins would be complete without some reference to those events in Salvation Army history which took him to the supreme international leadership of the Organization.

The days of 1929 when the High Council elected him to the Generalship were alive with discussion, and were not without sorrow and bewilderment. Much of the record is the work of people lacking personal experience in the matters of which they wrote. They relied for their facts on information given by others, and their colouring of the High Council story was often taken from the viewpoint of those with whom it was discussed. Edward Higgins, ever caring too little for himself, was content to leave matters there, even when statements were not too much in his favour.

Before he died, however, he agreed, responding to the pressure of friends, that some of his views might be published. But only on condition that controversy should be avoided and that no reflection should be cast on those who, during the important High Council period, expressed themselves as holding opposite views to his own and the majority of Army leaders at that time.

Often, when asked why he did not reply to reflections made upon his own integrity and sincerity, in the press and elsewhere, he declared that he would rather suffer misunderstanding and be misjudged than revive controversial matters which could not fail to produce unhappy results for the Army as a whole.

This attitude during his Generalship was not always understood by some of his staff, who were sometimes tempted to feel it was a sign of weakness. However, most of them later freely admitted his policy was the right one and the only way of maintaining the unity of the Army.

What in outline were the events leading up to the first High Council and what was the attitude of Edward Higgins, as Chief of the Staff?

Bramwell Booth's Generalship from 1912 was a period of outstanding leadership and brilliant advance for the Army throughout the world, coupled with a unity in its ranks and unstinted loyalty and affection for its leaders.

However, during the early part of 1925, murmurs of discontent began to be heard because it was thought by some that favouritism was being shown by the General in promotion and appointments, and because some felt that undue prominence was being given to members of the General's family. Chief of the Staff Higgins, with others, felt that such criticism of the General was unjustified.

There were other trends which troubled many thinking Salvationists. A study of The Salvation Army Deeds Poll of 1878 and 1904 revealed the tremendous powers centred in the autocracy of the General's position. The provision whereby a General chose his successor by placing a name in an envelope duly deposited with the Army's lawyers and opened at a General's demise, troubled some leaders as they looked into the future and saw possibilities of difficulties which might conceivably split the Army.

It seemed to many that the Army was too immense an organization to centre absolute control of its well-being in one man.

Unrest among the officers tended to increase rather than decrease, and ultimately found expression in a memorandum issued anonymously to all staff officers. Commissioner Higgins felt he could not entertain the slightest sympathy with such action, and both in conversation and correspondence condemned it. He resented some of the items in the memorandum, feeling them to be unjust and from some aspects untrue. Even in its reference to the method whereby a General chose his successor, a criticism with which he entertained some sympathy, he denounced the idea of working underground to achieve an end as entirely contrary to his sense of right and his idea of an officer's loyalty to a leader.

Bramwell Booth was deeply hurt by the memorandum, especially by the way it was issued. He could not believe that it expressed the feelings of the majority, although the fear that perhaps it did, and that he was in ignorance of the extent of the dissatisfaction, never left him. 'From that time', wrote Edward Higgins, 'his decision, his courage, his confidence was shaken, and it was revealed in many ways during the years that followed.'

60

All this can be well understood, since the memorandum had no precedent in Salvation Army history; it was an attack on the established order.

Whilst every effort failed to trace the author of the memorandum referred to (wrote General Higgins in some personal papers), it soon became apparent that whilst perhaps only a few would *express* sympathy with the method adopted by the writer, yet a large number were sympathetic with the grievances mentioned and the reforms demanded.

It was idle to close one's eyes to the ominous signs of a coming difficulty. The situation was discussed wherever a group of officers met together.

The policy adopted of treating the incident with some measure of contempt by making no reference to it in officers' councils or in official documents, did not result in quieting the agitation. 'What does it mean?' 'What is going to be done about it?' were questions officers asked of each other.

Through this unhappy period there were signs of a breakdown in Bramwell Booth's physical condition. Some thought that the General's health suffered as a result of a visit he paid in 1926 to the Far East.

Remembering the strenuous life Bramwell Booth had lived, the responsibilities he had carried from boyhood, the mass of detail which had come to him since the early years of the Army's existence, the financial worries and the cares associated with the formation of a new society which rapidly spread around the world, it was not surprising that, at 70 years of age, he would show signs of the wear of the years.

The unrest came into the open in 1927 when Commander Evangeline Booth, the General's sister in charge of the work in the USA, visited France at the request of the American Legion to address their annual convention held that year in Paris. After the convention she visited London and saw her brother. An interview on 11 October with him at International Headquarters informed him of her strong feeling that certain alterations were necessary in the Constitution of the Army as expressed in the 1904 Deed Poll, and presented him with a statement containing her views as to the changes desired, which statement became known as 'the Commander's 15 points'.

It was immediately after this interview, when Bramwell Booth sent for his Chief of the Staff to discuss its details, that Higgins made it clear that the request of the Commander for a change in the method of appointment of succeeding Generals had his sympathy. This was doubtless a shock to the General, for he preferred to think that in this matter as in others he and his Chief were in full accord, although there had never been any discussion of this particular subject between them.

Commissioner Higgins felt the General's position was extremely difficult, especially as he maintained his inability and unwillingness to make the suggested changes in the 1904 Deed Poll, believing, he declared, it to be his sacred duty to hand The Salvation Army's constitution to his successor unchanged.

Realizing the delicacy of the position, Higgins urged the General to relieve him of his position as Chief of the Staff and to select someone in entire harmony with his views, at the same time promising to accept any other position in the Army entrusted to him.

General Bramwell was unable to grant this request, urging that the Chief should stand by him. This the latter promised to do if it was understood that he would express no views contrary to his convictions. At the same time, he was willing to pass on the General's views, provided it was stated that they were the General's.

On two occasions when the position between the two men was at a stalemate, the Chief of the Staff reiterated his plea for relief, but his requests were not granted.

In May 1928 the General had a serious breakdown in health and complete rest with cessation from all business was insisted upon by his doctors. The General's absence from International Headquarters (his last appearance there was 12 April 1928) did not stop the spread of the movement for certain reforms, and from all parts of the world there came requests that the points raised by the Commander should be favourably considered by the General. He was too ill, however, to see most of these communications and probably never knew the extent of their demands.

Through the summer his health grew worse and those who wanted him to make reforms felt he would never be able to do so. Particular stress was laid upon the necessity for some new method of choosing the Generals of the Army. It was realized by those active in seeking this that unless it was accomplished in Bramwell Booth's lifetime, new and more serious problems could arise.

The General continued too ill to attend to any business and at the end of October, when there were no signs of improvement but rather the contrary, seven Commissioners demanded the calling of the High Council—a constitutional right—'for the purpose of adjudicating whether the General for the time being is unfit for office'.

The requisitioning Commissioners were: Samuel Hurren, Robert Hoggard, Charles Jeffries, David C. Lamb, Henry W. Mapp, Wilfred L. Simpson and Richard Wilson.

Their action was endorsed by the undermentioned retired Commissioners, who considered that in the circumstances the requisitioning Commissioners could have taken no other course: John A. Carleton, William Ridsdel, Mildred Duff, Adelaide Cox, Frederick de L. Booth-Tucker (Fakir Singh), William Stevens (Yesu Ratnam), Clara Case (Nurani) and William H. Iliffe.

The calling of the High Council came as a distinct surprise to General Bramwell Booth's family. However, the provision in the Constitution declares it to be the duty of the Chief of the Staff to call the High Council when requested to do so by seven Commissioners. Edward Higgins had no choice but to follow their wishes.

From the time of calling on 15 November 1928 to the assembly of the High Council at Sunbury Court on 8 January 1929, the Chief of the Staff strove to the utmost of his ability to maintain a fair and impartial attitude.

He constantly sought and secured advice from the solicitors of The Salvation Army upon new problems which faced him daily. He refused the use of any Salvation Army funds for propaganda purposes for either side. It was a period of extreme difficulty, emphasized by the continued illness of the General who, until a few days before the High Council met, knew nothing of its calling. The Chief consistently refused to discuss with the press anything to do with High Council business.

Naturally Salvationists all over the world were anxious concerning the turn of events; the rank and file could not, and at first did not, understand what it was all about. Some officers knew of the difficulties culminating in the High Council proceedings, but many were bewildered. Higgins issued orders that no officer should make any statement either in the press or from the platform. He felt it inadvisable for either side to say in public what concerned The Salvation Army in an essentially private way. Salvationists were urged to leave the entire matter in the hands of the Council, who would weigh all matters with equity and a supreme desire to safeguard the interests of The Salvation Army which they all loved so dearly.

In a statement in *The War Cry* of 5 January 1929, the Chief of the Staff called on 'every Salvationist to pray earnestly that God will overrule everything that is said and done for the glory of His name, and the furtherance, the world over, of the Army's work of carrying the message of salvation to the people'.

Undoubtedly grave dangers, with possibilities of rift and dissension, threatened the Organization at this hour. But the time of crisis became a time of prayer. All over the world Salvationists prayed that God would protect the Army and guide its leaders. Those supplications were answered. Though the Army was shaken it remained intact.

11

The Council meets

IT is not easy for a man to legislate against a friend, no matter how right and necessary the action may be; and it is doubly difficult when such a friend is a beloved and trusted leader whose armour it has been an unspeakable privilege to bear for a decade.

That was Edward Higgins' unenviable position between 15 November 1928, when duty demanded that he should call the High Council, and 8 January 1929, when it was officially convened.

But he had done what he conceived to be his duty and it was done in the spirit of love. Could a man do more? Perhaps not; but the situation caused him—to use his own words—'untold anguish'.

On more than one occasion he urged, through Mrs General Booth, that the General should meet the difficulties by making necessary reforms, which would satisfy the demands of the Commissioners of the Army and prevent action detrimental to himself. A few days before the High Council met, he wrote a final appeal suggesting once more that the General should promise not to appoint his successor but rather leave such appointment in the hands of others.

Knowing as he did the great importance Bramwell Booth attached to this power of appointment, Higgins outlined a scheme suggesting that the General should nominate three people as suitable to succeed himself. These three nominations were to be placed in separate envelopes. At the death of the General the first envelope would be opened and the Commissioners of the world informed by cable of the General's first choice. They would express agreement or otherwise. If a majority (to be decided upon) approved, then the person named would assume the Generalship. In case of the needed majority being lacking, the second envelope would be opened and the same procedure followed. If again the second name also failed to secure the necessary number of votes, the third envelope would be opened; and only if all three nominations were rejected would the High Council be called.

65

By this plan it was felt that a General would most likely nominate an acceptable person and at the same time retain a measure of power to choose his successor, yet not actually appoint him. Such a scheme, carefully drafted, would do away with the necessity of summoning the High Council too frequently, since voting could be by a carefully protected cable system.

'Alas!' wrote Edward Higgins concerning the suggestion, 'the scheme was returned with the intimation that it was felt the General would be unwilling to consider it.'

Many Commissioners urged the Chief of the Staff to assume the Presidency of the High Council, but he felt it would be wisest to attend only as a member.

Apart from opening proceedings with the song 'Mine to rise when Thou dost call me', leading prayer and reading Scripture, he took only a meagre part.

Commissioner James Hay, in charge of the work in New Zealand, was elected President, with Lieut.-Commissioner William Haines, Managing Director of The Salvation Army Assurance Society, as Vice-President.

Of the 64 officers summoned to attend 63 responded, the only absentee being Commissioner Wm E. Oliphant, who for health reasons was unable to make the journey to London.

The position of the Chief of the Staff was one of extraordinary difficulty. As F. A. Mackenzie points out in *The Clash of the Cymbals*:

> He felt himself under a double obligation. On the one side he was the General's chosen representative, called upon to act and speak for him to the Army, and as such it was his duty to do everything that he could to see that the General's cause obtained a full and fair hearing.
>
> On the other hand, as second-in-command, he owed his primary allegiance to the cause and not to any man personally. There was general agreement among even the most ardent reformers that Commissioner Higgins acted throughout this period with prudence, dignity and restraint. All that could be done for the General, he did.

Some things were said which hurt him sorely and he might have defended his point of view successfully and with ease; instead, he chose generally to be silent; and herein may be discovered the innate greatness of a man who was prepared to suffer and be misjudged, rather than provide fuel for fires that might be hurtful to others and harmful to the Army.

One of the initial acts of the Council was to send a message to General Bramwell Booth expressing affection and sympathy with him in his illness.

Throughout the proceedings there was sensed a deep love and solicitude for the General. How earnestly the Council sought to avoid the necessity of judging him unfit! Sympathetic minds and tender hearts hoped they might induce him to go out with flags flying, the recipient of every honour that could be accorded him and thus adequately crown the magnificent leadership of the years.

In this spirit they prepared a letter to him:

We are encouraged in submitting this resolution to you, by the remark made by yourself on the question of your retirement and contained in your letter to us.

We therefore beg of you to embrace the opportunity of relieving yourself of the burden which at your time of life has proved to be far too great and to retire from your office with full honours and dignity, and so emphasize once again the high ideals which you have so eloquently preached to us by word and example.

The cold phraseology of a formal resolution would certainly fail to convey to your mind the love and kindly feeling which were readily manifested during our discussion, and which accompany this proposal.

Now in your closing years, tired, frail and unable longer to lead us forward, we would tenderly urge you to relieve yourself of your impossible task and assure you that your place in our highest respect and our hearts' warmest affection is for ever unalterably fixed.

Then came the formal motion:

To place on record its high appreciation of the life and labours of the General and join with him in gratitude to God for his partial restoration to health, and express the hope that this improvement may be maintained.

The Council being, however, unable to see the practicability of the suggestion made by the General, and realizing that it is most unlikely that at the General's advanced age he can ever recover sufficiently again to take up the burden under which he collapsed, takes the opportunity of requesting him to co-operate with the Council in securing the future welfare of the Army, and to that end it resolves that, the General being, as his doctors assure us, capable of considering important questions and giving decisions thereon, the President, Vice-President and five members of the High Council be deputed to see the General and suggest that he now retire from office, retaining his title of General and continuing to enjoy the honours and dignities attaching thereto.

Amid scenes of deep emotion, the tenderly conceived retirement motion was voted upon.

Army leaders filed to the President's desk to sign the letter and wept unashamedly. Some felt they could hardly write their names. Said one: 'Forty years ago he encouraged me as a boy; now I ask for his retirement.' It was not until the Council had sung a hymn together, 'O God, our help in ages past', that hearts became more steady and emotions were under control.

Of the members 56 signed the letter; 7 were not in agreement.

It was about 10 am on Friday 11 January 1929 that the deputation from the Council, consisting of the President (Commissioner James Hay) and the Vice-President (Lieut.-Commissioner William Haines), Commissioners John Cunningham, Samuel L. Brengle, George Mitchell and Gunpei Yamamuro, with Colonel Annie Trounce, waited upon General Bramwell Booth at his modest seaside home at Southwold, Suffolk.

When they entered the sick room they were shocked by the sight of a gravely stricken man, wonderful still in spirit but woefully sick in body.

The deputation's official report read:

> The General seemed to remember us all and spoke a word to each, quite tenderly asking about wives, and casually referring to our work.
> The documents referred to were lying on the bed before him. He spoke of having read them. He said he had a great trust passed to him by the Founder and that the proposal we had made required time— 'I must have a little time.'
> Turning to the President, he said: 'The old General had a great fight for one-man control. You believed in that.'
> As it was evident the General could only keep his thoughts connected by our not interrupting him we withheld any remarks at this point.

He referred to his health and again to having received his trust from the Founder and from God. He said he realized what we were asking, and added: 'But I must have light to see what I must do and how I must do it. I have had some trouble in my soul. God has given me very gracious feelings in the years gone by. Perhaps He wants me to do without them now!'

We endeavoured to speak to him through his acousticon. He did not seem to catch our expressions, and Commissioner Catherine suggested that she should repeat our words.

She did so, but we were thinking the deputation was impressed that he was not quite following, or was not quite able to follow, our statement that the Council felt tenderly towards him and that they wished him to consider the document before him, and after taking a little time for consideration give us his answer.

The General went away from the subject, one would say, as if he had certain intentions in his mind to speak on other questions, and he followed, so it appeared, the preparation of his mind.

For example, he spoke of the new Denmark Hill building, asking us in general if we had been there. We intimated that we had not. He made some almost jocular remarks that Brengle would perhaps say it was too ecclesiastical, and Mitchell might say, 'What about Hoxton?' and Hay and Whatmore would say, 'I got the idea in Melbourne'. But this, however, was said very slowly.

The General still fingered the document, revealing his feeble nerve-distressed hand, and added, 'I must have a day or two to think'.

After making a further remark or two to the members of the deputation, it was apparent he had said as much as he was able to say.

Mrs Booth suggested to the General that he should pray with us, just as we were about to suggest the same. This seemed to give him a little refreshing of thought, and grip of his memory, and he prayed slowly but tenderly for 'These men and their families'.

He prayed that 'these men might act aright'. He spoke to God of his health, mentioning his hope that God would come to him quickly. He prayed for God's guidance in this matter and referred to his extremity, and that God might make an opportunity out of that.

He thanked God for the help already given him and used the expression, 'Help them to help me now and help me to do the right thing in the right way'. He also prayed for India.

The prayer—as were his other words—was slow and one would say an effort. The President started to pray for the General, and possibly not hearing, he started off again in prayer. Then he stopped and the President completed the prayer, after which the seven of us shook hands gently with him, kissing his hand and wishing him all blessing.

It was quite evident the deputation could not wisely stay longer.

The General's reply came on the following Tuesday, 15 January, and was disappointing to the majority of the Council members. Bramwell Booth felt he would be failing in his duty if he retired.

When the General's reply was received the Council adjourned to the afternoon. Everyone knew what was ahead and everyone mourned the inevitable.

While thousands of prayer meetings were held in Salvation Army buildings throughout the world that God would guide the Council in its deliberations and preserve the international oneness of the Army, the discussion on the General's health proceeded. The deputation's report greatly strengthened the view that it was hopeless to expect a complete recovery.

Soon after eleven o'clock at night the Council adjudicated that Bramwell Booth was 'unfit for office as General of The Salvation Army' and removed 'him therefrom'. Because of the formal manner of voting and the precautions taken, it was half an hour after midnight when the result was made known with the motion being carried by 55 votes to 8.

12

God's choice

THE weighty problem to be solved on Friday 18 January 1929 was, who would be Bramwell Booth's successor? But perturbing and disconcerting news interrupted the day's talks and consideration of suitable candidates.

A telephone message was received from the Chancery Division of the High Court of Justice, and afterwards due notice served, indicating that Mr Justice Eve had that morning granted a temporary injunction restraining the High Council from acting on its decision to depose the General and elect his successor until Monday. The application had been made on behalf of General Bramwell Booth and was based on the grounds that the Deed Poll of 1904 was not valid because a trustee of a charitable trust could not alter the trust at will, and the Council's procedure was a violation of the Deed Poll and contrary to the principles of natural justice.

Members of the High Council were distressed by the turn of events. No doubts had been entertained concerning the legality of the Deed Poll of 1904 since that had been drawn up by a trio of able lawyers which included Lord Oxford and Asquith, and Lord Haldane.

Weeks of delay with court proceedings followed. It was an irritating situation. The Council chafed at the need which kept them in London when their presence was so much required in their own commands throughout the world.

Mr Justice Eve asked the Council to adjudicate again the matter of the General's fitness after hearing counsel and other testimony on his behalf.

Following the lifting of the injunction the Council met again on 13 February and adjudicated Bramwell Booth unfit for his office for reasons of health.

The High Council then proceeded to the business of electing a new

General, and it soon became evident that the choice lay between Evangeline Booth and Edward J. Higgins, both of whom delivered a candidate's speech.

The result of the poll was declared soon after midnight, Commissioner Higgins being elected by 42 votes to 17.

The new General, standing high in the confidence and esteem of his fellow leaders, had without doubt added to his stature by a humility of spirit, poised reserve and kindly but statesmanlike reactions during the High Council proceedings. Salvationists around the world welcomed General and Mrs Higgins with affectionate acclaim and a moving and spontaneous greeting was given the General as he arrived at the International Headquarters, Queen Victoria Street, London.

Police were needed to deal with the crowds massed in front of the Queen Victoria Street building, yet no ceremony could have been less formal or more impressive. The General sprang out of his closed car and was surrounded by a 1,000 cheering saluting friends. Obviously touched by this warm expression of affection that no breath of winter could chill, he addressed them informally: 'You must all be as good as you can. You must all work as hard as you can. You must keep the flag flying as high as you can. Do good to all men, and let mercy and justice triumph throughout the world.'

During the next two weeks General and Mrs Higgins visited Clapton Congress Hall; Colston Hall, Bristol; St Andrew's Hall, Glasgow; Free Trade Hall, Manchester; Albert Hall, Nottingham; and the new City Hall in Newcastle upon Tyne. Without exception the buildings were too small to accommodate the eager crowds. Civic and religious leaders graced the platforms, bidding welcome to the new leaders and prophesying for the Army a speedy and happy recovery from its temporary difficulties.

General Higgins' first message to The Salvation Army world was under the caption: 'There must be no easing off.' 'More than ever', he urged, 'we need red-hot religion. The tepid, insipid and spiritless religion, of which we see so much around us, is rejected by God and despised by the people. We must set ourselves to produce in every corps, in every institution and at every headquarters, a larger and stronger band of men and women in whose hearts burns the living flame of divine love.'

The new General received many invitations to address influential gatherings. At the annual meeting of the Free Church Council held in the City Temple, London, a month after his election he received a tremendous ovation.

Paris was the first city to be visited outside Great Britain. In two Trocadero meetings 70 men and women knelt at the Mercy Seat. Later, during campaigns in Switzerland, at Zurich and Geneva, the number registered was nearly 700.

Campaigns in Scotland and motor tours among the smaller towns of south-west and eastern England reached great crowds. The constant speaking in the open air, however, was a great strain and brought physical injury from which the General suffered for the rest of his life.

During these infant months of the new regime some efforts were made through the press to discredit the Higgins administration. Stories of revolt and secession appeared in the news columns, without an iota of justification. A London paper went so far as to say that so deep was the Army involved in financial difficulties because of the falling off in donations, that The Salvation Army Assurance Society had come to its rescue with heavy loans. Needless to say this statement was as false as the others and the next day the paper retracted the statement and apologized for its insertion.

Ugly words such as 'vendetta' and 'victimization' crept into print as General Higgins was publicly accused of discriminating against the family of his predecessor. At first he chose to ignore such falsehoods and to treat them with the contempt they deserved; but when the furore increased rather than abated he faced the facts of every accusation and point by point gave frank answers in official releases to the press. This assured a quick termination to a campaign of vituperation on the part of some person or persons unknown.

The broadminded charity with which the new General met misrepresentation won the admiration of the world, as well as Salvationists of all ranks. He was a disarmer of prejudice and criticism.

He made it perfectly clear that he stood for a General with authority and power. No one during the nearly six years of his Generalship ever suggested that he had made election promises which he did not keep. Even those things he endeavoured to achieve and were not agreed to were most certainly for reasons beyond his control.

On Sunday 16 June 1929, General Bramwell Booth passed to his eternal reward. He was 'promoted to Glory'.

General Higgins was due to leave for Finland the following day, but immediately cancelled his arrangements to devote himself to plans for the funeral and memorial service, in co-operation with members of the promoted leader's family.

The body of Bramwell Booth lay in state at the Clapton Congress Hall and thousands paid their tribute in an impressive setting which epitomized thanksgiving for a great life and work.

The memorial service at the Royal Albert Hall and the remarkable funeral procession through the City of London to Abney Park Cemetery were occasions in which the esteem in which the late leader was held was demonstrated by Salvationists and the general public alike.

Soon after his election General Higgins appointed a commission of leading officers to advise him on the best arrangement for holding Salvation Army property and other assets in the United Kingdom.

This was followed in November by an International Conference of Commissioners summoned to London to consider certain amendments to the Trust Deeds of the Army, made necessary by the growth of the Organization and the changes which had taken place since its Trust Deeds were first drawn up, particularly as these affected the powers and prerogatives of the General; and to decide upon the best means for giving legal effect to such changes as might be agreed upon.

He also issued a manifesto to Salvationists throughout the world:

It is common knowledge that at the time of my election as General, I stated that in my opinion, three main reforms were required, and these I pledged myself to carry out. They were the abolition of the General's right to nominate his successor and the substitution of the method of election by the High Council; the fixing of an age limit for the retirement of the General in harmony with the existing regulations for the retirement of all other officers; and the substitution of a trustee company to hold the properties and capital assets of the Army in place of the sole trusteeship of the General.

It will be seen that these items curtail to a considerable extent the absolute powers hitherto placed in the hands of the General by the constitution of the Army. Resolutions to give effect to these three reforms, proposed to the conference by myself, were carried with only two (in one case three) dissentients among the 42 Commissioners present.

Eminent counsel advised the General that the only possible way to implement certain of the findings of the conference held in November, points mentioned also in his manifesto, was by Act of Parliament. Hence 'The Salvation Army Act 1931'.

Most Salvationists felt these changes to be beneficial to the Army, adding to its security and giving it greater permanence; but there was a small vocal minority in opposition, largely because they felt the reforms did not go far enough. Liberty was given to any officer to express his or her views, to the extent of personally appearing before the committees of both Houses of Parliament to oppose the Bill. The General was criticized by some for allowing this freedom of expression and others thought him unwise, but he himself declared: 'I shall always be glad that in this matter I permitted any who wished to do so to express their views.'

General Higgins also set up an Economy Commission in 1931, the terms of which were to examine Salvation Army workings and determine possible economies. Each section of International Headquarters was reviewed and all established methods carefully examined in the light of efficiency and economy. Sentiment and procedure had no part in the objective work of survey and the commission's findings greatly benefited the Organization.

In these and similar ways the General launched a new era of Salvation Army progress; his courageous decisions and policies resulting in major contributions to the Army's strength.

The passing of General Bramwell Booth created new and awkward difficulties for his successor. The former General's will showed the addition of a codicil, by which the arrangement that his successor in office should be his executor was cancelled, and three other executors were appointed.

This action prevented the property and assets of The Salvation Army passing over almost automatically to the new General as the new trustee. Instead the Army's material possessions were in the hands of three trustees named even though they had no responsibility for the direction of the Army.

It was an embarrassing situation, for the trust had become separated from the trustee and General Higgins found himself in an unenviable position.

Weary months passed before the condition was remedied. Indeed transfer was not made to the new General until Mr Justice Clauson gave judgement in the Chancery Court on 21 January 1930, establishing the validity of the 1904 Trust Deed, and of General Higgins' appointment as General.

To read the minutes of the proceedings taken before the Select Committee of the House of Commons on Private Bills, and to digest the evidence of General Higgins who appeared as witness before the committee for two days, is to recognize with new understanding the true stature of the Army's third General. In a distinguished and famous company of men he was not only the central but the dominating personality.

Said Sir Lynden Macassey, KBE, KC:

> He was an inspiration to all those with whom he came in contact. Had it not been for his conspicuous honesty and integrity of purpose which completely dominated the atmosphere of the Committee Rooms of the House of Commons and the House of Lords, the Bill which I had the very great honour of promoting for The Salvation Army would never have been passed.
>
> It was not the speeches of the counsel or the evidences of witnesses which secured its passing into law, but the convincing argument of General Higgins' own personality and character.
>
> The Committee felt that the welfare and future of The Salvation Army were transparently safe in his hands.

In another note of a later year Sir Lynden wrote:

> Great personalities have always made their impression on me; I suppose my Irish temperament has given me that sensitiveness. General Higgins was outstandingly one of them. His courage and his resolution at I suppose the most critical period in the Army's history was one of the most impressive things I have ever seen, also his charitable endurance of cruel personal misrepresentation. There was never a more magnificent exemplification of the attitude of our Blessed Lord Himself.

Eloquent tributes these, which expressed the thoughts of an ever-increasing body of opinion, appreciating the true worth of the character and leadership of Edward Higgins both as a Salvationist and as a world figure.

13

A campaigning General

WHEN General Higgins appeared before the House of Commons
Select Committee on Private Bills, in connection with The Salvation
Army Act, 1931, he gave a true idea of the demands of his office as
General:

> I was asked for some idea of the work of the General, and I requested
> that there should be prepared for me something showing my own
> work for the last year, which I do not look upon as extraordinary. I
> find I visited and had campaigns in Great Britain, Holland, Germany,
> Norway, Sweden, Finland, Denmark, South Africa and Rhodesia. I
> conducted 240 meetings in the largest halls that were available. I had
> 71 meetings with officers of The Salvation Army, at each of which I
> spoke on an average for one-and-a-half hours; that I travelled nearly
> 40,000 miles; that I had councils, at headquarters, of course, upon a
> thousand and one things; that at headquarters I had 1,000 interviews
> of more or less difficulty; that I had to write and do literary work for
> Salvation Army publications all over the world, and had constant
> demands also from the outside press; that I had to prepare and write
> messages for officers and gatherings at which I am unable to attend,
> in all parts of the world. The preparation for those meetings and for
> those gatherings I am sure everyone will agree is of no small
> moment.
>
> In addition, I have the presidency of the large life assurance society
> connected with the Army, I am chairman of the bank connected with
> the Army, the head of a printing trade establishment, director of the
> Darkest England Scheme and Trust; I have all the responsibility
> affecting the finance, property, appointments and the administration
> of the Army generally, and give the lead to the Army in the spirit of
> aggression and of sacrifice. I think a few years like that will take its
> toll.

Most certainly here is a programme that would drain the resources
of most men. Yet for nearly six amazingly wonderful years Edward
Higgins successfully met the demands of such days, with a success
explainable only by the fact that he lived, preached the evangel, gave
his directives, renewed his mind, did his business, in the wisdom and
power of God through Jesus Christ.

During these years one great accomplishment followed another. The amazing itinerary of events proceeded with scarcely a break, and jumped as nimbly from Newcastle to Nottingham, as from Camberwell to Cambrai, or from New York to New Zealand. Reports show meetings held within a few days in Toronto and Cardiff, Blackfriars and Basle, Stockholm and Southampton.

At all centres great crowds flocked to hear him, the Penitent-forms were crowded with seekers, and tens of thousands were converted. The record of the 1929–34 years shows such stirring reports as:

'Five hundred seekers at Zurich; 275 at Geneva; 245 captured in Berlin prayer battle; Copenhagen's 308; 200 seekers at Westminster; 500 at Finnish Congress'; and with most of the larger towns in the British Isles and many cities of the world included in a list too voluminous for this story.

About this time radio evangelism gained in importance. At least once a year the General broadcast over the facilities of the BBC, and as might be expected, from a Salvation Army studio: the Clapton Congress Hall with 3,000 present and a cadet songster brigade of 600 (in 1929), or the crowded Regent Hall in the West End of London. These were occasions always marked by decisions for Christ from among both the radio audience and those in the meeting halls. The General's rich, friendly voice was broadcast also from many other parts of the world.

Almost every year continental Salvationists benefited by their proximity to London and welcomed General and Mrs Higgins to lead their congress gatherings. The General made his first air journey when he conducted the Copenhagen Congress in 1932. Royalty and national and church leaders, with the important citizens of many lands, welcomed the Higgins, sought their friendship, presided at their meetings and pledged their support to Salvation Army endeavour. At the Founder's Centenary in the Royal Albert Hall in 1929, Britain's Prime Minister, Stanley Baldwin, brought the main address.

Newspaper reporters were generally kind to Edward Higgins. His sincere understanding and good stories won the press. They liked his *bonhomie*, co-operation and approachability, consequently, on occasion, they were not afraid to 'let themselves go'. The influential *Manchester Guardian* reporting on a 'tumultuous reception' to the General continued: 'Your newspaper reporter finds himself a trifle

79

embarrassed in the midst of proceedings which defy the utmost limitation of his everyday vocabulary adequately to portray.'

'He is a real happy warrior', declared a Glasgow newspaper of the General, reporting a luncheon occasion with Sir David Mason, Lord Provost of Glasgow. Another reporter wrote: 'As the train from Glasgow steamed into the Central Station there stepped buoyantly to the platform a man of commanding military personality and genial presence. He was General Edward J. Higgins, CBE, the newly-elected commander-in-chief of The Salvation Army, and at once you said, "Here is a man!"'

One of Stockholm's leading dailies, the *Dagens Nyheter*, wrote: 'It is not every day that someone steps out of the Central Station, opens his arms to the people and exclaims: "God bless you all. God bless Stockholm. God bless Sweden." It must needs be the Salvation Army General to do that. Only he would not be laughed at or told to go about his business. General Higgins came, he saw, he conquered.'

A Canadian newspaper man described the General as 'the very picture of energy and goodwill'.

In its column 'Londoners at Work' the London *Star* reported: 'His day starts at half-past six. "I breakfast at quarter to eight sharp," he tells us. "I like to make sure of that meal. I leave home at eight-thirty. I get to bed when I can. . . ." The General has one of the most comprehensive postbags in the world. . . . This is perhaps his secret; he does things heartily. Nothing is a task to this man. Heartiness sums him up after all. He is not deceived by any, but he gives a welcome to all. He has a keen eye and a laughing face. Shrewdness and kindness; strength and gentleness. . . . He has the confidence of thousands who call him leader.'

In Canada, the USA, Australasia, Africa and India it was the same happy story of a modest but manly Christian leader capturing the imagination of his friends from the newspapers so completely that they dramatized him, and that with a likeable naturalness and spontaneity.

Always an apostle of progress, the General believed in advance, not for the sake of advance alone, but that it might lead to victory against sin, suffering and for the cause of Christ.

During his Generalship nine new countries were opened: Tanganyika, Algeria, French Guiana, Belgian Congo, Hong Kong, Uganda, South-West Africa, Yugoslavia and the Bahamas.

On 8 July 1929 Prince George, Duke of Kent, opened the magnificent group of buildings at Denmark Hill, London, known as the William Booth Memorial Training College. Costing £371,000, it was planned by General Bramwell Booth. As Chief of the Staff, Edward Higgins played an important part in the scheme and as General saw it brought to completion.

In declaring the training college open His Royal Highness said:

> I trust that out of the hard work—and it may be the severe test in lessons of unselfishness and the knowledge of life's darker side which will be the lot of many who pass through the institution—will come good and the perpetuation of The Salvation Army.

Typical of social service expansions was the Men's Social Work hostel in the West India Dock Road in London's East End (a Scandinavian sailor's temperance home taken over by the Army). On the day of dedication Prince Bernadotte wired congratulations and Archbishop Söderblom of Sweden cabled blessings.

Overseas the General inaugurated numerous social extensions including, in December 1933, the famous City of Refuge in Paris, opened in the presence of M Albert Lebrun, ambassadors, cabinet ministers and members of the diplomatic corps.

From the record of crowded days the following paragraphs each reflect a facet of the General's activities:

In 1930 he led the largest young people's councils ever held in The Salvation Army up to that year: 2,500 attended from five London divisions and there were 358 seekers with 151 candidates for officership, in a remarkable day at the Clapton Congress Hall.

London contributed a moving spectacle in 1930 when 800 staff officers solemnly reaffirmed their convictions 'in respect of our most glorious faith'. On behalf of the staff council, the General, with the Chief of the Staff and leading Commissioners, placed their signatures to the 11 points of Salvation Army doctrine; 225 attended the Southern European Staff Councils in Amsterdam which followed.

At a Sheffield rally in 1931, the General swore-in 200 new soldiers and there were 135 decisions for Christ.

'Two days with God' held at the Westminster Central Hall were features of General Higgins' London programme. In 1932, 170 knelt at the Mercy Seat.

When the Kettering Corps was opened by Captain Higgins, 'the Army was given a year to live', but when General Higgins returned 46 years afterwards, the local Salvationists were 'at their wits end' to accommodate the crowds.

One of the memorable days of 1931 for the General was spent with 1,300 men of the social services in London.

In this same year General Higgins re-opened the famous Clapton Congress Hall. There were queues for each meeting of the day and great rejoicings over 60 people kneeling at the Mercy Seat.

General and Mrs Higgins were among the guests invited by King George V to the 1931 garden party at Buckingham Palace.

After conducting Denmark's 45th anniversary congress in 1932 the General was received in audience by the King of Denmark.

Celebrating his golden jubilee of officership with a rousing soul-saving campaign at Norwich, the Army's leader received congratulations from Sir Ernest White, Lord Mayor of Norwich, and Dr Bertram Pollock, Bishop of Norwich.

After seeing 234 people kneel at the Mercy Seat in the Berlin Congress meetings, the General was received by President von Hindenburg.

Returning from India in 1933, General and Mrs Higgins attended 10 Downing Street for an important private occasion convened by Mrs Stanley Baldwin, wife of the Prime Minister, and addressed by the Foreign Secretary, Sir John Simon.

During the Easter week-end of 1933, 7,000 people heard the General at the Good Friday 'Day at the Cross' in Clapton, while 5,000 attended the Easter Sunday meetings in Liverpool.

At the Swiss Ascension Day campaign in Zurich, the international leader reviewed 4,000 Salvationists on the march.

An interesting international week is revealed by an extract from the June 1933 diary: Thursday—present at opening of South Africa

House by the King. Friday—interview with the Maharajah of Travancore. Tuesday—addressed drawing-room meeting arranged by Lady Steel-Maitland and presided over by Sir Arthur Steel-Maitland. Thursday—left London for Oslo to conduct congress.

During 1934 the General conducted a 10-day evangelistic campaign in the principal towns of Holland.

In a series of remarkable summer campaigns lasting for four weeks, with the slogan, 'Make your holidays into holy days', the General met the people by visiting every leading seaside resort in England for beach meetings.

In days bulging with demands it was still necessary for the General to give time to literary work. Millions who might never hear his voice had to be given the opportunity to read his words. Edward Higgins was the last to lay claim to an iridescent pen; nevertheless, his simple, forthright writings—sane and sincere in their expression of eternal truths and Salvation Army principles—promise to stand the wear of the years.

His volume *Stewards of God* is a manual of sound advice and certain inspiration for everyone called to spiritual leadership.

With Edward Higgins, sanctified imagination had full play. If a new thought had a sound foundation, it was energetically translated into action. The operational rut never became a grave. Plans were not always spectacular but they were provocative of amazing effort.

In 60 meetings held during a strenuous eight-day campaign through the lowlands of Scotland, 'The General', reads the report, 'captured the heart of Scotland'. An urgent, virile evangel was declared and there were many seekers. A similar idea proved equally successful in Wales.

Commenced in 1929, the 'Days of Fire' held at the Royal Albert Hall, London, were pentecostal occasions which burned themselves into the memory and experience of thousands, and started trails of red-hot enthusiasm for the things of God which encircled the globe. At the first of these days there were 157 seekers. The Albert Hall authorities were co-operative in using the elevators to bring seekers from the higher galleries down to the Penitent-form in the arena. An amplifying system was used for the first time in a religious meeting in this building. On the day preceding Salvationists participated in a mammoth march through London followed by many massed open-air meetings all over the city.

Typical of great demonstrations of prayer, praise and practical religion were the Crystal Palace (London) field days.

In 1929, 35,000 Salvationists expressed their thanks to God for the centenary of the birth of William and Catherine Booth in 12 hours of imposing pageantry, joyous music and fervent worship.

Two thousand songsters sang and 100 bands played. With fluttering flags and banners bearing such phrases as 'Salvation in the slums', '10,000 hallelujahs for the Founder's life and work', 'Jesus never fails'—all branches of Army work passed in review in a colourful march past.

Concluding a memorable day with a Mercy Seat lined with praying people, the General declared amid scenes of moving consecration, 'So let us sacrifice and toil that the Army may march on!'

These Crystal Palace gatherings, although not always of the same magnitude, gained spiritual momentum with the years. How Salvationists delighted in their sacred influences! How they prized these opportunities of intimate association with their leaders! 'The merest glimpse of General and Mrs Higgins', reads a report, 'was enough to unleash a thunderstorm of applause.'

In 1934, following a 21-meeting day at the Crystal Palace, the General conducted a day of councils with the bandmasters of the British Isles, the last he was to lead before his retirement. There were tears in many eyes as Territorial Bandmaster Alfred Punchard expressed the affection of the 600 bandmasters present, while at the close of the day the General was accorded acclaim given to few spiritual leaders. A *War Cry* report of the occasion reads:

> Facing them for the last time as their General he commenced in subdued tones: 'I wish for you all that you might be filled with the Spirit of God.'

A bandmaster remembered:

> Praying tenderly over them all he committed us to God's loving care and with a smile of affection and a friendly wave of the hand, disappeared through a door leading from the platform.

We were moved and suddenly everyone commenced to clap. The torrent of sound continued. Our emotions were beyond the power of words and so we clapped and clapped long after he had gone.

There swelled up through the tumult the strains of the International Staff Band playing: 'God will take care of you'; and we ceased applauding to sing—that is, those who could sing.

Then we clapped again and would not be denied until the General returned to the hall and stood in silent acknowledgement of the tribute of love his bandmasters had paid him.

When he slipped out again it was with Lawley's last word on his lip, 'Faithful'. We stood for a moment and then departed silently to think upon the stirring messages of the day.

Toward the end of 1930 the General had just returned from a tour of Africa, and in London was confronted with the spiritual challenges of life in England. What could be done? The answer came on 6 November at a day of 'Power and Glory' held in the Royal Albert Hall, when the league of goodwill was launched with Hugh Redwood, well-known author and journalist, as its president.

Thus commenced an added ministry to the poor of the slums of the great cities, with spiritual and social service values beyond estimation. Hugh Redwood, self-styled 'Big Brother' to his slum sisters and the Army generally, attracted to the goodwill league many hundreds of lay workers of every class, who volunteered to give spare-time service in the slums under the direction of Salvation Army officers. His book *God in the Slums*, which has been reprinted many times, stimulated the interest of many thousands in this work.

In a few years this scheme of practical service to the needy but often very proud poor, captured the imagination of thousands of Army friends throughout the world.

When the General visited Dover for a week-end's meetings a car had been provided for his comfort and transport to and from the meetings.

'Why do you go to the trouble of arranging a car like this?' he asked.

'General,' came the reply, 'we feel that the best we can do for you is the least we should do.'

85

'I'm grateful,' said Edward Higgins, 'but we'll just forget the car tomorrow [Sunday]. You meet me at my billet and walk down with me.'

So the General walked to the meetings on Sunday, to the corps hall in the morning where a wave of consecrations followed the address, and to the town hall for the afternoon and evening gatherings.

On Monday morning the divisional commander and the commanding officer walked with the General to the railway station, where as they waited for the platform gates to open, he talked quietly with them about the psychology of soul-saving.

Canterbury Cathedral presented a remarkable scene on the afternoon of Wednesday 25 November 1931, when, for the first time in the annals of the cathedral, The Salvation Army was accorded its hospitality and, at the invitation of the Dean, Dr Hewlett Johnson, the address was given by the General.

Nearly 3,000 Salvationists, with bands playing and banners flying, marched to the sacred edifice where the customary evensong became virtually an Army meeting. In the cathedral where Thomas à Becket was martyred the 'Hallelujahs' of Salvationists blended with the 'Amens' of the churchmen.

Of the occasion a newspaper report said in description:

A Palestrina anthem, unaccompanied, ethereal; the sweetest singing of cathedral choristers. And then 'Austria', full-throated and glad-hearted. 'Glorious things of thee are spoken' with massed Salvationist bands to stir the blood and a minor canon beating time from the pulpit to the great gathering in the nave.

What contrast, and yet what harmony. There was that in Canterbury Catheral this afternoon which seemed to heal the divisions of an age.

When it was first announced that the Dean of Canterbury had invited The Salvation Army to worship in the world-famed shrine, and had offered its pulpit to General Higgins, someone, who signed himself 'Puzzled', wrote in pained protest to the local press.

He had his answer on this day when the Dean, in his scarlet vestments, escorted the General—whose uniform looked sombre by comparison—to the place of honour reserved for him among the attendant

86

clergy. He had it when, in rear of the main Salvationist procession, with its forest of blood-and-fire banners, the civic heads of Augustine's city—Mayor and Sheriff, with all their retinue—marched up the aisle in solemn state.

As for the congregation, it filled the place completely, so that many were forced to stand, or sit upon the steps that lead to the choir. And while the Salvationist element, of course, predominated—for General Higgins' followers had come from all parts of Kent and Sussex—there was a large admixture of Anglicans and Free Churchmen.

The Army spirit was there, and the spirit of the Church was there. As General Higgins declared, 'Unity does not necessarily mean similarity; and diversity is very plainly part of God's plan in nature.' In the course of his address he said: 'I feel sure I shall not be misunderstood when I say how deeply my emotions are stirred, not alone because of the associations of this building, but because of the significance of the service itself in which we have joined, thus exhibiting that unity of spirit and singleness of purpose which speaks of harmony in our separate efforts.'

'After the final hymn', reported a newspaperman, 'Salvationists streamed out across the Close, cheering the Dean, shouting hallelujahs to the General and then proceeded to hold open-air meetings all over the ancient city of Canterbury.'

The success of many a man pivots on the inspiration of his wife, and General Higgins was the first to acknowledge the vital part which Mrs Higgins played in his life and leadership.

Certain it is that few women could have been better equipped to be a General's wife, either by experience or personal talents.

A successful officer before marriage, she continued in active leadership throughout her wedded life and never flinched in taking any responsibility that would bring glory to Jesus and help to the people. Mother of seven children, she nevertheless made a record of achievement for God and the Army brilliant in her own right and illustrious with that of her husband.

As the wife of the General she supported him at all public occasions, accompanied him on his world-wide campaigns and had a definite and appreciated public ministry.

A great deal of her thought was naturally given to the women of the Army and of the world. As international home league president, she directed this powerful women's organization, comprising the nationalities of the world and dedicated to the betterment of the home and home life.

She also had the oversight of hostels for missionary officers in Great Britain and directed the War Graves' Visitation Department at International Headquarters.

This latter activity proved a service of inestimable worth, especially in arranging pilgrimages of remembrance. These enabled the relatives and friends of men who fell in the First World War to visit the graves of their dead on the battlefields of Europe. Service hostels equal in comfort to good class hotels were set up in Ostend, Ypres, Arras, Amiens and Boulogne, to accommodate visitors on very reasonable terms. These hostels formed the centres from which the pilgrims set out to visit the graves under escort of Salvation Army officers who were familiar with the country and its ways.

Searching for a soldier's grave that was but vaguely indicated by a number taken from War Office records was an errand beset with many difficulties, and more likely than not to end in disappointment. Thousands of heart-stricken parents (some of them aged and infirm), widows unfitted for the buffetings of life, and other relatives and dependents of the gallant men who lay buried in the fields of battle, availed themselves of the facilities created by the Army to view the ground which had been made sacred by a priceless sacrifice.

Mere words fail lamentably to describe the mingled feelings with which relatives gaze upon 'their' plot in 'God's acre'. But as the Salvation Army officer took the visitor by the arm and said gently, 'Shall we pray just here?' there was something that touched the heart. And as the tears fell upon the grave there seemed to enter the brighter spirit of gentleness and comfort which reassures and satisfies.

Richly endowed with personal qualities for this tender ministry, Mrs Higgins accepted this major responsibility for 15 years until she retired from active service.

Blessed is the woman who is more interested in getting results than in getting credit. Mrs Higgins was a Salvationist of that kind.

14

World travels

GENERAL HIGGINS now belonged to the world. His international spirit, tried in the crucible of deep conviction and hard-won experience, dared not now fall short of a world-wide ministry.

Woven therefore into a heavy schedule of business and public engagements in the British Isles, were frequent campaigns in the countries of Europe, as well as major periods spent in the United States, Canada and Newfoundland, and lengthy tours in South Africa, Rhodesia (Zimbabwe), Australia, New Zealand, India and Ceylon (Sri Lanka).

These were not only occasions for out of the ordinary public meetings but valued opportunities for a close examination and survey of Salvation Army policies, personnel, methods and organization. Cities and nations gave of their best in magnificent tributes of esteem to both The Salvation Army and its leaders. Moreover, each tour became gloriously sacred because of the large numbers of 'miracles of grace'.

At the first opportunity in 1929 General Higgins set himself the task of contacting as quickly as possible the Army's far-flung battle-fields. In his judgement, the Army could not be adequately led, and its bonds of unity maintained, from an office in London; this was possible only by the personal touch.

After a congress in Sweden, in late August, General and Mrs Higgins set off for Newfoundland and Canada. It was the first visit of a Salvation Army General to Newfoundland since the Founder's campaign of 1894 and no warmer official welcome could have been possible than that extended by the Governor-General.

Often the General deplored the fact, yet recognized the necessity, that some of his meetings were of a character calling for a recital of the achievements of the Army, with little opportunity to teach holiness and salvation. Whenever he faced a crowd he yearned for

Penitent-form results. As his diary reveals, he often wished he could have successfully emulated his predecessor, General Bramwell Booth, and combined a lecture with an evangelistic appeal. He seemed to find it difficult to do this, but he made brave attempts in various parts of the world, and over 600 people knelt at the Mercy Seat during the meetings in Canada and Newfoundland.

In South Africa in 1930 General Higgins was involved in 70 meetings in 47 days, and in Rhodesia (Zimbabwe) 3,000 Salvationists encamped near the Howard Institute for a congress. Some of the delegates from Northern Rhodesia (Zambia) had walked 300 miles to be present.

As the General looked out over the huge throng of Mashonas he exclaimed: 'This beautiful picture is impressed on my mind so deeply that no matter how long I live I shall never forget it: I think I shall think about it even in the next world.' 'I love you! We all love you!' he told them, his extended arms moving to encompass the dense multitude of Africans draping the slopes of that hollow among the hills.

The audience, all a-tingle with pleasure, found their leader a man of fatherly kindness, a happy, smiling, massive, deep-chested, commanding figure, yet without pomp or self-assertion. A paramount chief knelt at the Mercy Seat. Then with three other African leaders, who had knelt with him, led the way to the plaited-grass-walled registration room.

Leading citizens of every centre lost no time in commending and thanking the international leaders for the invaluable work of the Army, to which Edward Higgins invariably replied in subdued terms, resolute against an acceptance of personal praise, guarding himself against himself and shielding his comrades from the danger of forgetting the divine origin of their inward power. 'If Christ's avowed followers fail in their duty', he declared in Port Elizabeth, 'they will one day stand in His presence ashamed and bewildered. And from what would failure more surely come than from a slipping into the mire of self-congratulation?'

In 1932 Australians found that General and Mrs Higgins were people after their own heart. During the tour over 250,000 people attended the meetings and the press generously welcomed the General 'of this Army which knows no political party and is not circumvented by any ecclesiastical shibboleths; which goes down to the slums,

90

with its ministry of helpfulness and hopefulness; which rescues the perishing, raises the fallen, cares for the outcasts, and even in an important sense raises the dead'. Another reporter wrote of the General: 'He is blessed with the knack of immediately taking a personal interest in you—jovial and sincere, and has a breezy frankness that marks him as a fine personality, obviously a leader of men, he appears to have a complete mastery of whatever task calls for his attention.'

The General was impressed with the welcome he received everywhere and with the sight of hundreds of people kneeling at the Mercy Seat. He warned his listeners: 'Make your religion as beautiful as your country and your fruit and flowers! Let it be a happy religion! Make everyone want it!'

In Adelaide the General spoke against a prevalent evil. 'I am wholly against gambling,' he said. 'We should get what we pay for—and pay for what we get. It is not right that the individual should be enriched at the expense of the community. Gambling strikes at the root of sober life.' And later, commenting on the place of women in public life, he exclaimed: 'My only complaint against women in public life is that there are not enough of them.'

The General had come to Australia via a series of engagements in the USA and Canada, the Hawaiian and Fiji Islands and New Zealand.

An hour before he reached Auckland little tug boats filled with New Zealand Salvationists, flying their flags, with hallelujahs and music complete, steamed round the ocean liner. At night the Auckland Town Hall was crowded and the General's message was broadcast throughout the country.

In Invercargill, city of the British Commonwealth nearest the South Pole, the mayor—obviously a son of Scotia—in his speech at the civic reception, humorously remarked that if the Army had to elect a new General he could not understand why they had not chosen a Scotsman. In his reply the General informed the mayor that by the time he reached London again he would have passed through seven Salvation Army territories and in each of them a Scotsman, or a man of Scottish descent, was in command, so he thought they had their full share of top positions.

At a reception in Parliament House, Wellington, Colonel Joseph

Pugmire, well-known Salvationist soloist, who was ADC to the General, sang his solo, 'Sunshine on the hill'. Then he succeeded in getting the three political party leaders—the Prime Minister (Rt Hon G. Forbes), Mr Coates and Mr Holland—to sing the chorus as a trio, much to the delight of politicians of all shades of opinion. It was said to be the first known occasion on which they were all in harmony!

Always appreciating the value of a good story, the General used many an illustration, humorous and otherwise, which caught the imagination of the newspapermen who often featured them.

In London the General related he was served with a summons by the City of Birmingham and fined a pound for keeping a common lodging house in which, on a certain night, he had permitted 371 men to sleep, instead of the 370 for which the place was licensed. 'I was fined', he said, 'because I allowed one unfortunate fellow too many to sleep in that house. Next day I received hundreds of letters of protest against the fine—and they all enclosed a one pound note with which to pay it. I wished more summonses would follow, for I never got money [for the Army's work!] more easily and at less expense.'

Arriving in San Francisco on one occasion the General was told not to hurry from the boat as the mayor, who was to greet him, had another engagement in which he was to welcome the Crown Prince of Japan. The mayor was there, however, smart in his morning coat and high hat.

Just as he greeted the General one of the reporters asked: 'Mr Mayor, whom did you put on the topper for, the Japanese prince or the Salvation Army General?' To which the mayor replied: 'I put on the topper for the Japanese prince, but I take it off to The Salvation Army.'

Then there was the General's story of a man who, when questioned by a Salvation Army officer as to his plight, declared: 'I am one of the unhappy mediums. There is no hope for me. I am too heavy for light work and too light for heavy work.'

'Years ago in Petrograd,' said the General in another vein, 'I went to the British Ambassador and told him of my need for a lawyer conversant with the Russian law, yet speaking English. I was introduced to one such man and took three days of his time discussing important legal affairs. ———

'At the close of our business I asked him how much I was indebted to him. Imagine my surprise when he said: "Nothing to you. The Salvation Army can never be indebted to me, for years ago in Chicago when I was down and well-nigh out, they gave me aid and placed my foot on the first rung of the ladder which has led me to where I am today."'

One of the General's quaint stories concerned a problem girl, despair of many social service agencies, who was handed over to the Army.

The Army lassies did their best, but she created such turmoil and disturbance that at last they suggested to the person interested in her that they could do nothing for her.

In reply to their letter they received a telegram which read, 'God needs honouring'. They read it and felt rebuked, so kept the girl and she eventually responded to their love and consideration.

When the inspector interested in the case made one of his periodical visits they mentioned his wire. He declared he had never sent such a wire. So they turned up the evidence. 'It doesn't sound like me,' he said. 'I am sure I didn't send it.'

Looking up his files he found that the telegram he had sent read, 'Girl needs humouring', but an all-wise Providence seemed to have guided the telephone operator in adjusting the message to Salvation Army language, to read 'God needs honouring'. The error meant the salvation of the girl.

In November 1932 General and Mrs Higgins farewelled from the Royal Albert Hall, London, for a campaign in India and Ceylon (Sri Lanka); a campaign which commenced in Ceylon in December and finished in Bombay the following February. Nearly 6,000 people knelt at the Mercy Seat in the meetings of a tour which covered nearly 19,000 miles by steamer, train and car.

The welcome meeting in Colombo, Ceylon (Sri Lanka), was a pattern of acclaim to the international leaders repeated many times throughout the Indian sub-continent. The élite in Ceylonese and European life were warm and cordial in their greetings. People of numerous nationalities and various beliefs listened to the General's words. In Colombo, for instance, there was the Sinhalese with his tortoise-shell hair comb, the Buddhist with his shaven head, Tamils, Parsees, Malaysians, Afghans, Burghers and Europeans.

Notwithstanding the great heat and the noise of whirling fans, both General and Mrs Higgins spoke with great freedom and power. Among those who knelt side by side at a crowded Penitent-form were a well-known church worker and a Buddhist who had walked 54 miles to be present.

Ten thousand people greeted the visitors in their first meetings in Southern India. In the congregation was seen the simple loincloth of the poor and low caste as well as the gorgeous and heavily jewelled attire of the wealthy. Sense of time was lost amidst the rejoicings of the vast audience. A high government official felt it was the nearest approach to Pentecost that could be imagined.

People from the villages, Salvationists with their timbrel bands, singing their native Indian songs and shouting their hallelujahs, gathered in Nagercoil—15,000 of them. This crowd was dwarfed, however, at a Sunday morning meeting at Tiruvilla where the congregation numbered upwards of 20,000 people. Here in picturesque language an address of welcome was read by a leading Brahmin. 'In this soul-stirring and inspiring meeting to check the enthusiasm was like trying to keep back the tide,' read a local newspaper report.

Early in the morning of the day before Christmas 1932, a reception was accorded the General at the Army's criminal tribes settlement at Stuartpuram. For a mile before his train reached the station cheering guards of honour lined the railway track, singing and clapping their hands. The settlement drum and fife band led the way to a large pandal and a meeting for over 3,000 criminal tribesmen.

The population of the Bapatla Leper Colony was cheered by the General's friendly words.

Then penetrating deep into the rural life of the land, the General visited a Hindu community of 3,000 souls. Here a man clad only in a simple loincloth handed over land valued at Rs 10,000, as a site for a new Salvation Army hospital.

In Calcutta General and Mrs Higgins attended a state banquet with their host, Sir John Anderson, Governor of Bengal, at Government House. The Viceroy, Lord Willingdon, with Lady Willingdon was present and the Army's leaders were the guests of honour for the occasion.

While the General was speaking in officers' councils in Calcutta, a murmur of translation was heard. In one part of the building his words were being translated to officers from the Lushai Hills and Assam; in another the interpretation was for the benefit of Bengali officers; in still another section the delegation from Orissa speaking the Oriya tongue were made to understand. Yet the audience, deeply affected by their leader's words, responded in the spirit of noble courage to his every challenge.

Of Mrs Higgins on this occasion a correspondent wrote: 'I remember Mrs Higgins spoke on the power of prayer. Very apt in her illustration, she said: "When I am burdened with the responsibility of some great gathering, I say to the General: Now you must pray for me. Get down upon your *two* knees and pray; no half-hearted *one* knee praying!"'

'Hallelujah! Hallelujah! I've still got it on my lips and in my heart,' exclaimed the General on arrival in London, where he found a great crowd of welcoming Salvationists at Waterloo Station. 'Hallelujah,' international word of praise, linked India to England, as indeed it links the entire Salvation Army world.

15

Honours for a warrior

IN early May 1934, General Higgins announced his retirement from active service to become effective later in the year. Thus he adhered to his statement of February 1929, when asked by the High Council to assume the Generalship, that he would not promise to continue in office after 70 years of age.

Although a large number of Army leaders throughout the world urged him to swerve from that promise, early in 1934, between sessions of a Spiritual Day at the International Training College, he felt obliged to consult Dr Hope Gosse, Harley Street heart specialist, and later was examined by another physician. In both cases the verdict was that he must relinquish heavy duties. Thus he felt compelled to accept the doctors' unfavourable diagnosis and adhere to his original plan to relinquish office.

But he was a spiritual campaigner to the end. The months between May and November were crowded with meetings in the towns of the British Isles as well as the leadership of important congresses in Denmark, Sweden and Finland.

Characteristically, in August he called the Army to prayer—prayer for the High Council and its important task of selecting the Army's new commander-in-chief. His stirring message, published in all editions of *The War Cry* throughout the world, ended appealingly and impressively with the words: 'Jesus *loves* to answer prayer.'

Thus toward the end of August 1934 Salvationists held a special day of petition which produced probably the largest and longest prayer meeting the world has ever known. It began in New Zealand and proceeded without a break in the countries of the world until it concluded in Hawaii. The world belonged to the Army and the Army belonged to the world, in the special sense of this sacred day.

The record of the six years of the General's leadership is one of amazement. Not only did he successfully pilot the Army through a stormy period of its history, maintaining its vital international spirit of Salvationism unimpaired, and reinforcing the essential principles on which his two great predecessors had built a religious and social service force which served the world, but he also carried out a tremendous personal programme of evangelism.

Visiting 22 countries, some European lands several times, he travelled not less than 220,000 miles. He was received by heads of state of each country visited, with two exceptions through their absence at the time of the General's visit. He was heard over the radio on 58 occasions.

Without ostentation and with the minimum of fuss General and Mrs Higgins travelled the world in the spirit of simple service and dignity.

In Stockholm the General suffered an acute attack of lumbago requiring vigorous treatment to alleviate the pain, but he used a hard high chair and carried through the entire schedule of meetings. There were no complaints. He smiled his broad friendly smile despite acute discomfort. He was that kind of man.

The response to the Higgins' leadership by world figures and the general public, as well as Salvationists everywhere, was as remarkable as it was gratifying.

Three typical occasions suffice to illustrate the point: the opening of a hostel for women by Queen Mary; a luncheon given in the General's honour at the Fishmongers' Hall, London; and the General's retirement and farewell meeting at the Royal Albert Hall.

Even a modicum of imagination is sufficient to lend significance and high drama to the opening of the Salvation Army shelter, accommodating 305 women, in Finch (later Hope Town) Street, Whitechapel, a needy spot in London's East End.

At three o'clock on 9 December 1931, amid a display of flags giving colour to a sombre area and through a guard of honour consisting of Army lassies, Her Majesty Queen Mary arrived to declare the institution open and was received by a Somerset boy, Edward Higgins, now General E. J. Higgins, CBE.

How little did the Somerset lad imagine during that night of spiritual battle in Bristol, more than 50 years previously, that such

97

an honour would come to him. He had renounced every thought of personal gain and had 'bet his life on God' in a spirit of utter abandon and irrevocable consecration.

Moreover, here was the once despised, persecuted and misunderstood Salvation Army welcoming to Whitechapel, place of its birth, the noblest in the land—leaders in society, church dignitaries and important civic personages, as well as a vast crowd of sincere friends and supporters.

The building itself was also typical of Salvation Army enterprise and another example of the unexpected which so often occurs in the organization's work. As General Higgins said in his address to the Queen:

> Your Majesty may be interested to know that the building you are about to declare open was originally a county council school, vacated because of changed local conditions, and sold to us by the London County Council in a rather dilapidated state for £8,500.

> To the uninitiated it appeared impossible to utilize such a building for the purpose of providing a home for the poor and homeless women of the neighbourhood, but The Salvation Army has become so accustomed to the conversion of the most unlikely human derelicts into happy and rehabilitated men and women, that it is perhaps only natural that in the realm of derelict buildings too our architects have been encouraged and inspired to believe that all things are possible.

After Her Majesty had declared the new hostel open and the Bishop of Stepney had offered prayer, she graciously inspected the premises, particularly the beds, one of which was uncovered at her request in order that she might examine the bedding. She discussed with the General the provision of recreational facilities for the women. Later the Queen was presented with a volume containing photographs of the hostel, but the gift which delighted her most was an envelope containing £25, handed to her by one of the workmen who, with his fellows engaged in the reconstruction of the building, had collected this sum to provide the women with Christmas Day festivities.

Almost every calling, strata of society and profession, including the Royal Family, the Church and the State, united on 5 July 1932 for a luncheon in Fishmongers' Hall, London, to pay an extraordinary tribute to General Higgins and to bid him (with Mrs Higgins) welcome home after his tour of the USA and Australasia.

The Prince of Wales sent a message conveying his good wishes, adding:

> I myself have been much impressed, during my various overseas tours, with the valuable work The Salvation Army has been carrying on for so long in distant parts of the world.

Writing of the event, Hannen Swaffer said:

> A great City luncheon took place yesterday, with the lord mayor in the chair, officially, and with civic dignitaries and nation-wide celebrities of all sorts present—and yet without any turtle soup.
>
> There was no champagne and there were no fat cigars. Indeed, nobody smoked, not even a cigarette.
>
> More than that, the only drink was thin lemonade and thinner water, except that, at the end, the guests had a wild time with small coffee cups.
>
> Gone for a while was all the traditional pomp and luxury of the City. It was a welcome home to General Higgins of The Salvation Army, who had just come back with his wife from an Empire tour.
>
> And so there were actually references to the gospel of Jesus Christ and the fact that the General during his tour had the joy of seeing over 1,700 men and women publicly confess their need of salvation by coming to the Penitent-form, in the presence usually of thousands of people.
>
> The Lord Mayor of London, Sir Maurice Jenks, presided, the Lord Bishop of London said grace.
>
> A brilliant address by the General was warmly received, in which he revealed the generosity of the railways and steamship companies toward The Salvation Army. In a tour of 34,000 miles free passage had been provided almost all the time.

When on the afternoon of Thursday 1 November 1934 General and Mrs Higgins retired from active service in a huge farewell meeting at the Royal Albert Hall, London, it was a royal ending to a distinguished career.

The Duke of York (afterwards King George VI) presided, accompanied by the Duchess and supported, as the *News Chronicle* pointed out, 'by the Ambassadors or Ministers of 23 different countries, three Cabinet Ministers, eight Members of the House of Lords, a group of Members of the House of Commons and dignitaries and leaders of almost every denomination, including the Bishop of London (who read part of Psalm 103), the President of the Free Church Council, Prebendary Carlile of the Church Army, Dr Campbell Morgan, Gipsy Smith and Mrs George Cadbury of the Society of Friends'.

The London *Times* commented on the singing by the congregation of 'the joyous opening song, "God is Love"'.

Dr Archibald Fleming, head of the Church of Scotland, remarked of the occasion: 'I hardly think that there is anywhere short of a royal court where such an imposing array of foreign ambassadors and ministers could be mustered as you have secured for this great occasion. The list is eloquent of the world-wide regard for The Salvation Army and its work and not least for General Higgins.'

The Duke of York referred to the great interest which the Royal Family had always taken in The Salvation Army, and emphasized the great claim which the Army made upon the regard of all sincere and thoughtful people, because it helped undoubtedly to make more tolerant religious opinions and class distinctions. 'I believe', he added, 'there is today more mutual sympathy and understanding, nationally and internationally, and The Salvation Army, among other religious and philanthropic bodies, has had a full share in bringing that about. General Higgins represents in himself those qualities of friendliness which belong, especially, to The Salvation Army.' That afternoon gave an opportunity to extend to him the heartfelt gratitude of those who have benefited by, and been strengthened by, the advice and guidance of the General and his loyal supporter, Mrs Higgins.

Outstanding tributes and good wishes followed from Dr J. H. Rushbrooke, President of the Free Church Council; Commissioner Charles H. Jeffries on behalf of Salvationists everywhere; Lady Simon; and General J. C. Smuts.

Said General Smuts: 'Our hearts are filled with gratitude today that General Higgins, at a very critical time for The Salvation Army, saw his job there, fulfilled his task and today hands it over to his successor in the condition in which he does.'

'By his wonderful tact, extraordinary patience and consummate skill,' declared Commissioner Jeffries, 'General Higgins has guided the Army through its difficulties, kept it marching in the right direction, leaves it today in healthier and happier condition than he found it. During his command it has maintained its unity—one in heart and purpose as never before. He has preserved its doctrines and teachings, and maintained its high standards of service and sacrifice.'

'The main contribution of the Army to the Churches is surely that it has recalled to us the fact that religion is of supreme importance,' was Dr Rushbrooke's warm tribute. 'The Army has never been merely a philanthropic body; it has from first to last laid stress upon the central message of the gospel—"The power of God unto salvation"—on the adjustment of the far deeper malady of sin; not on a social service programme, but on a saving Person.

'In Edward Higgins the spirit of the Army has found worthy embodiment. It was good indeed that a man such as he is has been called to lead it.'

Lady Simon said in part: 'We are here dedicating ourselves afresh to the work of service. The idea of The Salvation Army is of service. It is inspired by the thought that everyone of us has a piece of service to do, and that discharge of duty to others is that which enables us to discover the melody of life. When I pay a visit to a Salvation Army home and see the never-ending, unostentatious kindness given to the broken-hearted, and to those whom we call down and out, it reminds me of the words of Wordsworth in which he describes that best part of a good man's life—"those little, nameless, unremembered acts of kindness and of love".'

For the General the occasion was an opportunity to give an account of his stewardship. This he did in a way which stirred the great audience to its heart depths.

Giving God the glory and expressing gratitude for loyal helpers throughout the world, the General pointed out that despite the economic slump which claimed a large part of the years of his command, not a single ameliorative centre of the Army had been abandoned.

Included in an avalanche of tributes was a message from the General-Elect Evangeline Booth saying: 'I pray fervently for the General as he lays his burden down, but it is necessary that he pray much harder for me, for I am taking it up!'

Prime Minister J. Ramsay Macdonald thought: 'General Higgins' services to the Army in a difficult time are worthy of the gratitude of everybody who cares that all influences for good in these days should be supported with whole-hearted earnestness.'

The Rt Hon Stanley Baldwin declared: 'No one knows better than I the difficulties with which he has been faced in the last six years, or appreciates more fully what he has done for The Salvation Army, not only in this country but all over the world, and no one wishes him more heartily God-speed.'

Lord Lang, Archbishop of Canterbury (Cosmo Gordon Lang, and later Baron Lang of Lambeth), wrote in eulogy: 'His great experience, wide knowledge and devoted enthusiasm have made him a most valuable servant of the whole community. I pray that in the years that may yet remain of his long and useful life, God's peace may rest upon him.'

Thus did the world honour the Army's third General, humble and sincere follower of Jesus Christ, who combined the attributes of simplicity and efficiency with intrepid courage as a leader, and possessed deep spiritual resources that enabled him to lead The Salvation Army successfully through a challenging, stormy period of its history without loss in prestige, character or service.

At night the General led a 'Battle for Souls', in a building so crowded that the meeting began some time before the advertised hour.

As a postcript to the Royal Albert Hall day is a simple experience which greatly impressed a young corps officer. 'At the end of the day,' he related, 'I was walking along the corridors, when a door opened immediately ahead of me and the General stepped out. His face was burdened. My heart went out to this great man who had done so much for our beloved Army, so I came quickly to attention, saluted and said with sincerity and fervency, "God bless you, General!" I can never forget the rapid change of his grand countenance and the glorious smile he gave me, as he shook my hand and said in his rich voice, "God bless you, Captain!" Had I been a personal friend the greeting could not have been more cordial. Such was the impressive charm of this great Christian.'

A few days later General Higgins met his International Headquarters officers for a final gathering. Toward the end of his address he urged them to maintain Army principles and doctrines. The 20th century presented new difficulties, not so easy to combat. Salvationists had to fight not mobs, but unbelief. They no longer had prejudice to overcome; instead they must be uninfluenced by applause.

'God's power is ever the same,' he concluded. 'Have we the courage as of old, the willingness to suffer, the readiness to fight? Some say "No"; but I believe that is a slander on the young officers of the Army.'

Then followed a final Sunday at the Clapton Congress Hall, which included a broadcast service in which the General delivered a fiery address using the verse, 'I am the way, the truth, and the life'. 'There is no going without the way,' he said; 'no knowing without the truth; and no living without the life.'

On his last day at International Headquarters the BBC provided him with an opportunity to say farewell to all his friends in the British Isles.

'My wife and I can say that our hearts are full of love for all,' said the General. 'We are thankful for the guiding and sustaining hand that has led us, as we have striven to do God's will. We shall retain the same Salvation Army spirit, and we are both determined that the remainder of our days shall be spent to the same end in the blessed cause to which they have been devoted during the last 50 years.'

This day was naturally a time of many finalizations, but the General planned to leave quietly at the usual hour, feeling the final farewells had been said. But when he reached the lobby of the original 101 Queen Victoria Street he found a great crowd spilling over into the street, so police were on duty to make room for the traffic. All had gathered to say 'Goodbye and God bless you!' Edward Higgins was deeply moved, and a few moments later left the building to face the future, a retired General, henceforth to serve as a true soldier.

From the many tributes which the General received is the following typical expression from Commissioner William McIntyre (then Territorial Commander for the USA Central Territory):

Honours have not tarnished his spirit. He has kept his soul blameless, meting justice and mercy to all. He is void of all that is preten-

103

tious, and free from the arrogance which often spoils leaders. As he retires he is universally loved as are few men of world eminence.

He was elected to the Generalship at a time when there was need for understanding, tact, forbearance, impartiality; and General Higgins met the demands of the day with holy fortitude, unimpeachable integrity and utter selflessness. His balance and poise, his unrelenting war on evil and his Job-like patience when severely tried, have made him outstanding among the cavalcade of splendid souls who comprise the leadership of this Army.

For nearly six years now he has been God's builder. He has been wise in statesmanship, free from fads and as wide as the horizon in his sympathy.

He relinquishes his task with a good conscience. He leaves the Generalship with a rainbow of hope encircling the Army. And none can gainsay the fact that much of the glory of this ribbon of hope has come from the colourful personality, beautiful Christian spirit and red-blooded Salvationism of General Edward J. Higgins.

16

Final promotion

WITHIN a week of his retirement Edward Higgins was taken seriously ill. While resting at Margate, mysterious fevers asserted themselves; the doctors were puzzled, but withheld their diagnosis. A specialist was called in and thought an operation necessary. But the General gave a very emphatic 'No!'

For a month he was a sick man. He lost 30 pounds in weight, which, however, proved beneficial. Then to the joy of his friends, who feared the General would have little or no retirement, he recuperated enough to be able to travel and early in January 1935 left for the USA. A further medical opinion in New York urged a warm climate, so to Miami, Florida, where health was restored and he was able to proceed to California to visit an officer son.

During these weeks there were many talks with friends and family members as to the best place for a permanent home, but the summer of 1935 was spent mostly at the Army's Monmouth Beach, New Jersey, home of rest. Not far away is the Methodist community of Ocean Grove, with its great auditorium for camp meetings which attract the best speakers of the world. To the joy of American Salvationists, the General was the speaker on Salvation Army Sunday.

At the end of the summer General and Mrs Higgins responded to an invitation to spend the winter in Sebring, Florida, and before the spring arrived they had decided to settle in this picturesque city resting in the centre of a belt of orange orchards. An unpretentious home was secured on the lake shore.

The Higgins became soldiers of the Sebring Corps but found it in rather a discouraging condition. Only 11 people were present at their first Sunday morning holiness meeting. It was a challenge to the new soldiers, but they gave all their energies to help make improvements. Mrs Higgins arranged Sunday morning speakers and soon filled the hall. From the first she was also active in home league affairs. Only six women attended her first meeting but soon the membership had soared to over 100.

The 'Happy Hour' was inaugurated at the citadel each Friday night, featuring a songster brigade, organized chiefly among retired officers. This became one of the finest vocal groups in Sebring.

The General also initiated a movement to raise $10,000 for the reconstruction of the corps building, sadly in need of repairs and enlargement.

The former commander-in-chief and his wife were in great demand for public meetings and officers' councils throughout the country. The General commissioned cadets, and led campaigns at the Old Orchard, Maine, camp meeting. He also led the 50th anniversary celebrations of the Army's work in the Argentine, as well as important gatherings in Brazil, Uruguay and Chile.

It was, however, in the corps at Sebring that the General found an outlet for his keen intellect and vigorous salvationism. His life was ever satisfyingly full.

In April 1938 the Higgins celebrated their 50th wedding anniversary, a gala occasion for Sebring; and in 1944 Salvationists joined in recognizing Edward Higgins' 80th birthday, when messages were received from all over the world.

About the time of his fourscore years, the General's health began to fail. His long years of strenuous endeavour, coupled with the weakness of body in early years, showed themselves in physical ailment which gradually made it more difficult for him to walk. Nevertheless, he refused to miss the Sunday morning holiness meetings or to allow Mrs Higgins to lessen her activities in the home league. With physical strength and ability to use his limbs ebbing, however, the General's last public meeting was conducted on Easter Sunday, 1945.

Sebring in the summer is hot and trying for an ailing man, so a move was made to Toronto in 1945. Canadian Salvationists welcomed the Higgins with enthusiasm. Frequently Toronto's fine corps bands marched into the street where the General and his wife had their humble rooms, to play a spirited march and the beloved songs of the Army. There was always an adequate reward—the General's warm greetings and broad smile.

106

Early in 1946 because the General needed more elaborate care than Mrs Higgins was able to give, they journeyed back to the USA to the Army's convalescent home at High Oaks, Watchung, New Jersey, where, except for a few weeks in a New York hospital, the grand warrior spent his sunset days.

High Oaks was a pleasant place and was made hallowed by the General's presence. When other convalescent officers spent a period at the home, they found the indomitable, happy spirit of their former leader the best tonic for their recovery.

'I am now in my 81st year, and I am compelled to acknowledge infirmities that put an end to many activities that have filled my life with so much of joy and satisfaction,' he declares in a precious document, written in a trembling hand, and discovered among the General's personal papers, probably his final written message and personal testimony.

'I am no longer able to walk, it is not possible to write, as once was my pleasure, reading has become difficult, and other ailments have made a change in my usual method of life. But I feel no disappointment, nor have I a single complaint to make.

'In these days when reflection can have such full play, there is too much for which I am grateful to allow one word of grumbling to cross my lips to anyone, or a thought of it to occupy my mind for one solitary minute. No doubt there are desires that I would have liked to have had gratified, but thoughts of what I have had forbid me to be other than full of gratitude.

'I should have been glad to have visited my native land again. We never thought when we left it 10 or 11 years ago, we should never return. The war is largely responsible for this. How I hate war! There must be an end to what the world has suffered during the past years. Of course, nations will disagree, but I am full of hope that some other way may be found of settling their disputes.

'I would have loved to witness again Penitent-form scenes at the Royal Albert Hall, the Westminster Central Hall, the Clapton Congress and Regent Halls in London, the large halls in Great Britain and the world, as God permitted me to see in earlier days.

'What a joy to shake hands once more in this life with those who fought with me in some of the battles in the past.

'But I have no complaint. I think of the opportunities of life. I remember the satisfaction of these years of a devoted wife, of loyal children, of splendid comrades all over the world.

'Many have asked me if I regret any step taken at the crisis of the Army and I can truthfully reply in the negative. To me there can be no doubt but that the action taken in those critical years was for the best and the better foundation of the Army for the future. I can remember nothing I said that I regret. Perhaps, as I said at the time, in the future some further alterations may be required and if so I hope there will be men and women then as courageous as those of the past who will do as may be felt wise and best for our Army.

'The great doctrines and principles of The Salvation Army are as essential today as ever. No change in a world so full of change could warrant any alteration in these. I thank God today I was never tempted to swerve in these particulars, nor did I ever hear anybody suggest it, when other changes were being considered.

'The great doctrine of holiness as preached by the Army's Founder and later by General Bramwell Booth is as much a part of God's great purpose for man today as ever. We must preach it and practise it. With my latest breath I would urge all, officers and soldiers, to declare it. I pray nothing may be allowed to interfere with our resisting every effort to change its meaning or experience.

'In these days of change I see such a danger of the anti-worldly spirit losing its front place in Salvation Army life. How often I have seen hours spent with penitents at the Mercy Seat getting them to part with signs of worldliness on their attire before leaving the Penitent-form. That spirit does not change with the passing of time, it is as important as ever.

'Then in my reflective moods, I fancy (am I correct?) that sometimes I detect that in our social service work an absence of spiritual effort which has made the Army's social work the wonder of the world. I know that in some countries governments are introducing methods which often run across some of our principles, but I say without hesitation where this is the case I would prefer to do without social work, than try to run it without God and religion. What sights I have seen of hundreds of social cases, men and women, saved and become happy Salvationists! This is our justification for entering into social service work.'

Edward Higgins was promoted to Glory from the quiet of the New Jersey countryside on Sunday afternoon, 14 December 1947, at the age of 83. Salvationists of the world were typified in the salute of America's National Commander, Commissioner Ernest I. Pugmire, at the impressive service to a soldier held in the Centenary Memorial Temple, New York City; the thoughts of tens of thousands from every continent centred in the Salvation Army plot at Kensico Cemetery, just outside New York City, where the Chief of the Staff, Commissioner John J. Allan, conducted a committal service notable for its spirit of victory and triumph, thankfulness and praise.

Having brought the Army successfully through the storms, the storm pilot himself had safely reached the eternal harbourage of the just.